Living Faiths

Islam

Stella Neal

Series Editor: Janet Dyson   **Consultant:** Robert Bowie

OXFORD
UNIVERSITY PRESS

OXFORD
UNIVERSITY PRESS

Great Clarendon Street, Oxford, OX2 6DP, United Kingdom

Oxford University Press is a department of the University of Oxford. It furthers the University's objective of excellence in research, scholarship, and education by publishing worldwide. Oxford is a registered trade mark of Oxford University Press in the UK and in certain other countries

© Oxford University Press 2013

The moral rights of the author have been asserted

First published in 2013

British Library Cataloguing in Publication Data
Data available

978-0-19-913807-4

10 9 8 7 6 5

Paper used in the production of this book is a natural, recyclable product made from wood grown in sustainable forests. The manufacturing process conforms to the environmental regulations of the country of origin.

Printed in India

Acknowledgements

The publishers would like to thank the following for permissions to use their photographs:

Cover: dboystudio/Shutterstock; **p8:** Art Directors & TRIP/Alamy; **p10l:** Louise Batalla Duran/Alamy; **p10r:** Art Directors & TRIP/ Alamy; **p14:** World Religions Photo Library/Alamy; **p15l:** mrfiza/ Shutterstock; **p15r:** ersoy emin/Alamy; **p20:** Rahhal/Shutterstock; **p22:** Richard Levine/Alamy; **p24:** Bettmann/CORBIS; **p27:** Getty Images; **p34:** With kind permission from www.muslimhands.org. uk; **p36:** AFP/Getty Images; **p39:** Zurijeta/Shutterstock; **p40:** Nigel R. Barklie/Rex Features; **p41:** Shoosmith Multicultural Britain Collection/Alamy; **p43:** Catchlight Visual Services/Alamy; **p44:** LUKE MACGREGOR/Reuters/Corbis; **p49:** Robert Harding Picture Library Ltd/Alamy; **p50:** VikaSuh/Shutterstock; **p51:** Ian Miles-Flashpoint Pictures/Alamy; **p53l:** DAVID MOIR/X02060/Reuters/Corbis; **p53r:** DYLAN MARTINEZ/Reuters/Corbis; **p54:** AFP/Getty Images; **p57:** Janina Struk/Alamy; **p58:** NASA/JPL/California Institute of Technology; **p60:** Firdia Lisnawati/AP/Press Association Images; **p61:** Getty Images; **p64t:** WireImage/Getty; **p64b:** Pictorial Press Ltd/Alamy; **p65:** Peter Forsberg/Alamy; **p67:** aberCPC/Alamy; **p68:** Marco Di Lauro/Getty; **p69:** ImagesBazaar/Getty; **p71:** Jeff Morgan 13/Alamy; **p72:** Diverse Images/Getty; **p75:** Getty Images; all other photos by OUP

Illustrations by: Gareth Clarke

From the author, Stella Neal: I would like to thank Mujtaba Nazir for his research contribution and his guidance. I would also like to thank my two patient children, William and Elsie, who are around the same age of the readers of this book. Without their love and support this would have been impossible to achieve. Also to my Muslim friends who fed me, remained excited when I was bogged down with hard work and reminded me that my duty was to please Allah with this book. Finally, the experience that goes into this book has been gained by learning from the pupils I teach at Slough Grammar School. Marshallah, their sharing and expression of love for Islam has driven my curiosity as I hope it will yours.

OUP wishes to thank the Yassin, Ahmed and Atcha families for agreeing to take part in the case study films and to be photographed for this title. We would also like to thank Professor Ghulam Sarwar of the Muslim Educational Trust for reviewing this book.

We are grateful for permission to reprint extracts from the following copyright material:

Extracts from The Qu'ran are taken from the following translations: *The Qu'ran* Sahih International version (Al Muntada al-Aslami, 2004) *The Qu'ran* in English and Arabic translated by Yusuf Ali (Sh Muhammad Aswat, 1975) *The Noble Quran* translated by Dr Muhammad Muhsin Khan: (Dar-us Salam Publications, 1994)

We are grateful for permission to reprint extracts from the following:

The Way of the Prophet: a Selection of Hadith by Abd Al-Ghaffar Hasan, translated and edited by Usama Hasan (The Islamic Foundation, 2009), reprinted by permission of the publishers, Kube Publishing Ltd.

Beginners Book of Salah by Ghulam Sarwar (8e, Muslim Educational Trust, 2008), reprinted by permission of the Muslim Educational Trust.

Although we have made every effort to trace and contact all copyright holders before publication this has not been possible in all cases. If notified, the publisher will rectify any errors or omissions at the earliest opportunity.

Contents

Introduction

What's it like to be a Muslim?

The *Living Faiths* series helps you to learn about religion by meeting some young people and their families in the UK. Through the case studies in this book you will find out first-hand how their faith affects the way they live and the moral and ethical decisions they make. The big question you will explore is: What does it *mean* to be a Muslim in twenty-first century Britain?

The icons indicate where you can actually hear and see young people sharing aspects of their daily lives through film, audio and music. This will help you to reflect on your own experiences, whether you belong to a religion or have a secular view of the world.

Key to icons

Image gallery   Audio   Film   Worksheet   Interactive Activity

The Student Book features

Starter activities get you thinking as soon as your lesson starts!

Activities are colour coded to identify three ways of exploring the rich diversity found within and between faiths. Through the questions and activities you will learn to:

- **think like a theologian**: these questions focus on understanding the nature of religious belief, its symbolism and spiritual significance
- **think like a philosopher**: these questions focus on analysing and debating ideas
- **think like a social scientist**: these questions focus on exploring and analysing why people do what they do and how belief affects action

You will be encouraged to think creatively and critically; to empathize, evaluate and respond to the views of others; to give reasons for your opinions and make connections; and draw conclusions.

Useful Words define the key terms which appear in bold, to help you easily understand definitions. Meanings of words are also defined in the glossary.

Reflection

There will be time for you to reflect on what you've learned about the beliefs and practices of others and how they link to your own views.

Assessment

At the end of each chapter there is a final assessment task which helps you to show what you have learned.

Ways of helping you to assess your learning are part of every chapter:

- unit objectives set out what you will learn
- it's easy to see what standards you are aiming for using the 'I can' level statements
- you're encouraged to discuss and assess your own and each other's work
- you will feel confident in recognizing the next steps and how to improve.

We hope that you will enjoy reading and watching young people share their views, and that you will in turn gain the skills and knowledge to understand people with beliefs both similar to and different from your own.

Janet Dyson
(Series Editor)

Robert Bowie
(Series Consultant)

Meet the Families!

In this book, you will meet several young Muslim families from across the UK. You can read about their thoughts and views on various topics covered in the book, and also watch their full interviews on the *Islam Kerboodle*.

The Yassin family

Ibrahim and Sarrah live in Newport, Wales with their parents. They are all very involved with the local Muslim community and enjoy many different activities. Ibrahim and Sarrah play the piano and cello respectively and Sarrah also sings. Ibrahim enjoys the sport of archery, and paint-balling.

The Ahmed family also live in South Wales, and are neighbours with the Yassins. The children, Rahaf and Saad, enjoy reading. Saad likes playing football. They also enjoy going to the cinema.

The Ahmed family

The Atcha family

Abdul-Hakeem, Ali, Noah and Safeeya live with their parents and grandparents in Bolton. They visit the local mosque for prayers daily. Together, the children like to take part in many activities such as biking, badminton, swimming and gymnastics. They spend time with their extended families and take walks around the west Pennine moors.

Overview

To be a Muslim means to submit to the way of Allah (God) – not only by having faith in Him, but by carrying out five compulsory actions (known as The Five Pillars). These are set out in the Islamic holy book, the Qur'an.

Muslims believe that whatever happens in this life is a test, and that the next life is more important. Prayer is central to Muslim life: Muslims pray five times a day, attend Friday prayers at the mosque, and also make personal prayers. Muslims believe that they have a duty to care for others, so they give regularly to charity. They fast during the day at the period of Ramadan. The festival of Eid-ul-Fitr, which ends Ramadan, is a joyous occasion for the whole community.

The story of Islam begins with Adam and Eve. Muslims can trace important influences on their beliefs and practices over centuries of holy writings, as well as through the teachings of Prophets like Ibrahim and Isma'il. These form the foundations of Islam, but it was the birth of a boy in Makkah in 571 ce, that was to be the start of Islam as it's practised today by millions of people across the world. That boy was to become the Prophet Muhammad.

Muhammad's childhood was often hard, and he was orphaned at the age of six. As he grew up, he became known as Al-Amin – the Trustworthy – and was called to become a Prophet when he was forty. You will find that the story of how Allah spoke to Muhammad through an angel to reveal his Word is an exciting and dramatic one.

Even when he was violently attacked by his opponents, Muhammad lived justly and peacefully. He treated his enemies with mercy and forbade his followers to attack first. He protected women and made the welfare of the community a high priority. He expected fairness amongst his followers and honour in business dealings. In this way, he set the rules for a society by interpreting the word of Allah as it was revealed to him. He practised what he preached and so became an example for all Muslims. In fact, many Muslims say or write 'peace be upon him', sometimes in Arabic, after the name of the Prophet Muhammad, as a sign of respect.

Muhammad taught people how to behave, and what the consequences would be for disobedience. He emphasized that all will be judged on the Last Day – those who have disobeyed will be punished in hell, while those who have followed 'the Straight Path' of Islam will enjoy perfect peace in paradise.

It is often the case that people confuse cultural practices with religion. The ways in which Islam is sometimes represented in the media can lead people to associate it with violence. This book challenges some of the stereotypes about Muslims and gives you an opportunity to raise critical questions and to make informed decisions about some important issues.

Finally, for Muslims, Makkah is the holiest place on Earth. All Muslims pray that one day they will be able to visit Makkah for Hajj – to purify themselves and to show their love and commitment to Allah. Journey with us now from this – the centre of the Islamic world – to the heart of Islam. Enjoy your journey.

1.1 Who are Muslims?

Learning Objectives

In this unit you will:

- investigate what makes someone a Muslim
- evaluate the qualities Muslims value in a person
- reflect on what makes you who you are.

Starter

- Write down everything you associate with the word 'Muslim'. If you're not sure, think about what you would need to ask to find out more.

In order to find out about what it means to be a Muslim, you will need to consider what they look like, what they do, and what they believe (as shown in the Venn diagram).

Some Muslims are easy to recognize, because they wear special Islamic clothing, such as the **hijab** for some women or **mosque clothes** for men. Although some Muslims choose not to wear Islamic clothing (because of their particular culture or beliefs), most Muslims try to wear 'modest' clothes.

The most important Islamic belief is that there is one God – **Allah** – and Muhammad is the messenger of Allah. Muslims declare this belief using the **Shahadah**.

The words of the Shahadah may seem simple at first, but it reflects many key beliefs.

a

Look like: modest clothes, may wear the hijab, mosque clothes, influenced by culture

Do: avoid harmful things, develop good qualities, want to please Allah

Muslims

Believe: One God Allah, Muhammad is Messenger of Allah, Shahadah

b The Shahadah in Arabic calligraphy

? Can you think of any other words you could add to this Venn diagram?

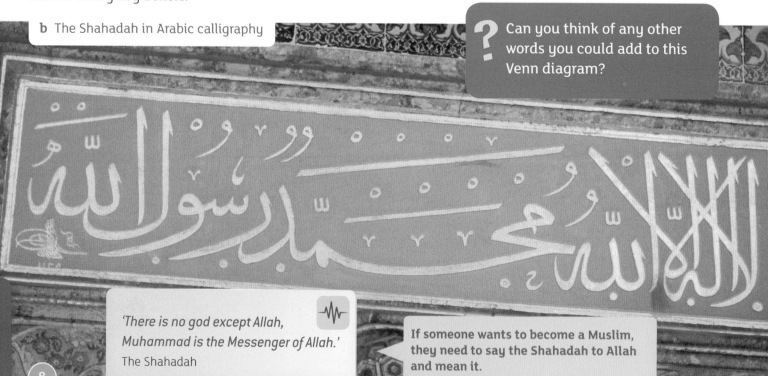

'There is no god except Allah, Muhammad is the Messenger of Allah.'
The Shahadah

If someone wants to become a Muslim, they need to say the Shahadah to Allah and mean it.

? This is the Ahmed family, who live in Newport in Wales. What do you think this family is like? What do you think they believe? How can you tell?

Muslims believe that Muhammad, a human being, was the Messenger of Allah and that Allah sent the holy text, the **Qur'an**, as a special message to Muhammad. He was given the task of bringing people back to the belief in Allah. Muhammad helped people to understand the true meaning of Islam.

Muslims believe that to do what Allah wants may be hard in this life, but that Allah knows best. 'Submitting' to Allah brings 'peace', as their destiny is in His hands.

SLM

iSLam   saLaaM

Submission   Peace
(to do what God wants)

c Have you ever wondered where words come from? In Arabic, the language of the Qur'an, some groups of words come from the same starting point – like branches growing from the trunk of a tree.

Activities

1 Which do you think is most important – how you look, what you do, or what you believe? Which do you think is the most important characteristic of a Muslim? Discuss with a partner.

2 Using the words of the Shahadah, and other information from this unit, design a poster which shows what Muslims believe.

3 'Sometimes we should just accept that others know best.' List times when this is and is not true and give examples.

Reflection

Look at the Venn diagram on the opposite page. What do *you* look like, do and believe?

1.2 Who is Allah?

Learning Objectives

In this unit you will:

- explain some Islamic beliefs about Allah
- investigate why Muslims do not draw pictures representing Allah
- evaluate the difficulty of developing certain character traits.

Starter

- Name a famous person and create a quick 'fact file' about them. How well can you really 'know' someone you have never met?

Muslims want to know Allah and many believe that everyone is born with the desire to be with Allah. But many Muslims also believe that Allah cannot be fully understood because he is greater than human understanding, and cannot be seen. So, how is it possible for them to get to know Him?

Muslims learn about Allah's qualities by reading and reciting the 99 names they have for him as stated in the Qur'an. Some examples include: Allah – the Greatest Name; Ar Rahman – the Gracious; Ar Rahim – the Merciful; and Al Khaliq – the Creator.

'No vision can grasp Him, but His grasp is over all vision: He is above all comprehension [understanding], yet is acquainted with [knows] all things.'
The Qur'an 6:103

Useful Words

Subhah These are beads used to keep count of personal prayers. Some have 99 beads and some 33, so they are especially useful for reciting the 99 names of Allah

a Sometimes Muslims use **subhah** to keep track when they are reciting the names of Allah.

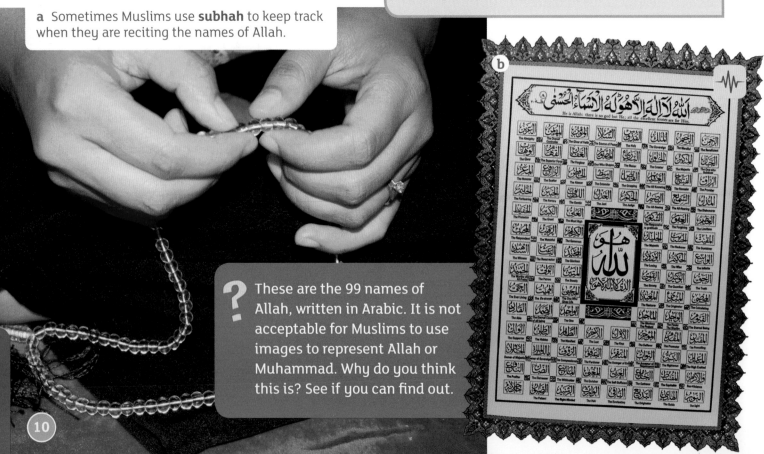

b

? These are the 99 names of Allah, written in Arabic. It is not acceptable for Muslims to use images to represent Allah or Muhammad. Why do you think this is? See if you can find out.

Al Khaliq (the Creator)

Muslims believe that Allah created everything.

'And We have already created man and know what his soul whispers to him, and We are closer to him than [his] jugular vein'
The Qur'an 50:16

? The jugular vein is the main vein in someone's neck, and if it is damaged, a person could die. What do you think it means to say that Allah is closer to humans than the veins in their necks?

Al Muhyi (the Giver of Life), Al Mumit (the Taker of Life)

These names show that Muslims believe their lives are in Allah's hands, and that no one can change the time of their birth or death.

As Sabur (The Patient One)

Even though Allah set out a way of life in the Qur'an and sent many prophets including the Prophet Muhammad to guide people, Muslims believe that people continue to disobey Him. They believe that He continues to show patience towards humans.

Ar Rahman (the Gracious), Ar Rahim (the Merciful)

Muslims believe that people often struggle with what is right, but as long as they try hard to be good and have the right intentions when they do things, Allah is merciful when they get it wrong.

c Many Muslims repeat Ar Rahman and Ar Rahim every time they pray.

Activities

1. Think of someone you look up to and suggest some different names or titles you think sum up their qualities.

2. Think about these two statements:
   • Muslims believe Allah is unseen and unknowable.
   • Muslims give Allah many names.
   How would you respond to both statements?

3. a Choose two of the names of Allah and write, in your own words, what you think these say about Muslims' beliefs about Allah.

   b For each one, talk with a partner about your own response to that idea of who Allah is.

Reflection

Think about situations where you might need to show patience, mercy and grace. How easy or difficult is it to develop these qualities, and why?

1.3 A Whole Way of Life: Submission to Allah

Learning Objectives

In this unit you will:

- examine the belief held by many Muslims that everything comes second to their faith in Allah
- explain the belief that Muslims should submit to the will of Allah
- reflect on what the driving force is in your life.

Starter

- Think of ten words that help to explain trust.

The most basic Islamic belief about Allah is tawhid, which means oneness or unity. This means that Allah is the one and only universal God. Muslims believe that if Allah exists, there can be nothing like Him – so nothing is more important than Him.

If Muslims become proud or envious or selfish, they break tawhid. This is because they are putting themselves before Allah, or taking credit for things that have happened because of Him. Most Muslims will say 'masha allah' (because of Allah) when they describe someone's good characteristics, or 'alhamdulillah' (thanks to Allah) when something good happens. When they do something, they will often do it in Allah's name by saying 'bismillah' (in the name of Allah) before they start.

? Imagine if, for the rest of your life, you thanked or acknowledged another person when something good happened. How would you feel?

a Believing these things about Allah fills many Muslims with a sense of awe and respect.

all-powerful

all-knowing

gave people life

made people who they are

Allah

made the wonders of the universe

sees all that people do

judges people after death

The Qur'an is believed to be the actual words of Allah, which means that Muslims try to follow the teachings of the Qur'an in every aspect of their lives. Many believe that everything comes second to trying to do what Allah wishes, or accepting the path Allah has put them on. This is called submission.

Muslims respond to the greatness of Allah by building their whole lives around Him. They believe that doing this will result in giving them many good qualities:

- They will not be arrogant, because they know that everything they have comes from Allah.
- They answer to Allah for their actions, so they take their responsibilities seriously.
- They develop courage, because they know that they must accept tests from Allah.
- They have self-respect, because they depend on and fear no one but Allah.

Reflection

'People put their trust in a God because other people often let them down.' Agree or disagree?

Case Study

Mrs Yassin, the mother of Ibrahim and Sarrah, says that if Muslims follow 'the prophet of Islam and what he said, and what he did', then they will truly have grasped 'the meaning of Islam', which is 'peace with yourself, peace with your soul, peace with your family, peace with the environment, everything'.

? Why do you think Mrs Yassin believes that submission brings peace? Do you think Muslims could find this peace if they do not do everything that is required of them?

Activities

1. Write down three advantages you can see in the Islamic belief and practice of submission to Allah.

2. Consider these quotes and write about two of them. Include your own thoughts and what you think an Islamic response might be.
   a 'We should learn to trust no one but ourselves'
   b 'Freedom can be a burden'
   c 'We can only find true peace if we get rid of all our selfishness'.

3. In small groups, share what you already know of Islam and, in the form of a poster, present your ideas about how submission to Allah's will might affect: food, dress, relationships, parents, charity, prayer and any other aspects of life.

4. 'Submitting to the will of Allah would limit a Muslim's free will.' Consider arguments for and against this statement.

Learning Objectives

In this unit you will:

- develop an understanding of how Muslims see Allah's involvement in their daily lives from birth onwards
- learn how belief in Allah turns into action
- evaluate the idea that people are born with the desire to be with Allah.

Starter

- If you could go back in time to your own birth, what would you whisper in your own ear? Why?

When a Muslim baby is born, the first words he or she hears – whispered by a male relative or **imam** – are the words of the **adhan** (the call to prayer). This is done because Muslims believe that everyone is born with the desire to be with Allah.

In Islam, the parents' job is to make sure that the child knows how to maintain their natural connection with Allah, and so a Muslim child is taught many rituals and practices with the aim of helping him or her keep Allah in mind.

For example, many Muslim parents ensure that their children learn to read the Qur'an in Arabic, by taking them to special lessons after school each day. They also take them to the mosque regularly to meet with others and worship Allah (see Unit 2.5).

? Look at this image and discuss your initial impressions with a partner. What different factors might influence this child's faith?

a A male relative whispers the adhan into a newborn baby's ear.

Useful Words

Adhan When a person called the Mu'adhin says a prayer calling Muslims to pray; in many countries it is played through loudspeakers from the minaret (tower) of a mosque, so that everyone can hear, stop what they are doing and pray

Imam A religious leader in Islam

If you listen to Muslims talking, you may hear them say phrases like 'inshaa Allah' (if God wills it) or 'alhamdulillah' (thanks to Allah). Saying these phrases can help some Muslims to keep Allah in mind. Muslims also try to keep in mind Allah's wishes in the way that they behave.

Another important way Muslims express their beliefs about Allah is through calligraphy, or decorative writing. Many Muslim artists express themselves by painting calligraphy.

b Many Muslims have calligraphy as decoration in their homes.

'The strong man is not the one who wrestles another to the ground: the strong man is the one who controls himself when angry'
Hadith

? Put this quotation into your own words. How far do you agree?

c

? This image is by Islamic graffiti artist Mohammed Ali. Why do you think he has chosen this form of expression? What does it communicate?

Activities

1 Create a birthday card for a young Muslim child. In both the design and wording, make sure that you reflect an understanding of the religious responsibilities that they take on from their parents at this age.

2 With a partner, make a list of questions that you would ask a Muslim of your age about his or her relationship with Allah.

3 Muslims believe that people have an instinctive need for Allah, but others would argue that a person is only influenced by how they are brought up. Write a script for a discussion on this topic between a Muslim and someone who disagrees with them.

Reflection

Think about the good and bad things that you have done in your life. What influenced you most at those times? What would influence a Muslim?

1.5 What are the Five Pillars?

Learning Objectives

In this unit you will:

- learn about the significance of the Five Pillars for Muslims
- develop an understanding of and explain how Muslims put the Five Pillars into action
- analyse why some duties are easier to follow than others.

Starters

- What are the five most important things you do in your life? Draw around your hand and write one on each finger.

The Five Pillars of Islam are five 'duties' that Muslims believe they are required to do. The word 'pillars' is used because, in the same way that a building is held up by pillars or supports, these actions are the basic building blocks of Islam.

Each pillar is a different way in which to worship Allah. The Five Pillars were practised by the Prophet Muhammad, who is believed to have been taught about them by an angel (Jibril). Muslims believe that carrying out these actions both follows the Prophet's example and also strengthens their love for Allah.

? Put the Five Pillars in order of which you think should be most important for a Muslim and explain your reasons.

Shahadah: The first basic duty of a Muslim is to make a declaration that there is no God but Allah, and that Muhammad is Allah's Messenger.

a For Muslims, worship through the Five Pillars builds on the foundation of faith.

Shahadah | Salah | Zakah | Sawm

Sawm: Fasting for the month of Ramadan. Many Muslims do not eat or drink from first light of dawn to sunset. (See Unit 3.3)

Salah: Prayers five times a day at set times, which change with the seasons. These prayers are performed in a set way. (See Unit 3.1)

Zakah: Giving 2.5% of your annual savings, usually donated each year. It is given up to acknowledge that Allah is the real owner of their wealth and Muslims simply have use of it for a while. (See Unit 3.2)

Case Study

Ibrahim Yassin is in his last year of school in Newport, Wales. He first said Shahadah on his sixth birthday.

'I'd said it before but was just repeating the sounds and actions. The first time I said it and meant it, my dad told me that I was part of 1.6 billion other Muslims and I remember feeling very serious about that'.

> **?** How do you know when you've tried your best to fulfill your duties, and it's OK to give up?

While Ibrahim firmly believes that the Five Pillars are very important, and that all Muslims should try hard to do all of them, he also thinks that 'some are difficult, like Hajj. This requires physical strength, and the money to get there.' He says that if a person is ill or lacks the money to undertake Hajj, 'there's no penalty'. He says of the Five Pillars: 'they're all important, but not always easy.'

Reflection

Which would you prefer: to follow a clear set of requirements, or to do things your own way? Why?

Hajj: A pilgrimage. Muslims should try to go to Makkah (the city where Muhammad was born) at least once in their lives, if they are able. The annual Hajj is the biggest gathering of people on Earth. (See Unit 3.4)

Activities

1. Write a postcard to Ibrahim Yassin, above, asking him questions about the Five Pillars and what they mean to him. Create a relevant design on the other side.

2. Which personal qualities would a Muslim have if he or she followed the Five Pillars? How else could these qualities be developed? Discuss with a partner.

3. 'People should be allowed to worship in any way they wish.' How would you respond to this comment? Consider arguments for and against.

4. Can you think of 'pillars' in your own life? Something: you give; you always remember; you want to do once in your life; you do every year; you do several times a day.

What do Muslims Believe?

Objectives

- Demonstrate knowledge of key aspects of Islamic belief in Allah.
- Show understanding of the relationship between Allah and Muslims, and how this relationship is strengthened by practice.
- Reflect on your own opinions about young children following rituals.

Task

Draw on your learning about Muslims' relationship with Allah to debate the statement: 'Belief in Allah is all a Muslim needs.'
Do you agree or disagree? Explain your reasons.

a Prepare: In groups of four or five, identify and prepare evidence that supports each side of the argument.

b Debate: Use your prepared ideas to support what you say in a class debate about the above statement. You need to make sure your arguments are persuasive.

A bit of guidance...

This task allows you to show that you can interpret a range of beliefs, evaluate the importance of beliefs and actions, and work out how a Muslim would interpret teachings in their everyday life.

Making the declaration of Shahadah is what makes someone a Muslim. You need to look at the different ways in which Muslims show their Islamic identity, in order to decide whether it's simply enough to declare Shahadah.

Hints and tips

To help you tackle this task, you could do some of the following:

- Use and expand the Venn diagram in Unit 1.1.
- Watch the video clips on the *Islam Kerboodle* to see what Muslims say about believing in Allah or research online.
- Interview a Muslim in your school.
- Explore how the Five Pillars impact individuals and communities.

Guidance

What level are you aiming at? Have a look at the grid below to see what you need to do to achieve that level. What would you need to do to improve your work?

	I can...
Level 3	• use some religious words to describe what Muslims believe about Allah • explain some of the actions Muslims should take.
Level 4	• use more religious words to describe Islamic beliefs and actions • list key Islamic actions, including the Five Pillars • give an example of how performing certain duties affects Muslims' lives.
Level 5	• use an increasingly wide range of religious words to describe Islamic beliefs and actions • give one reference to scripture to support my work • suggest reasons why not all Muslims behave in exactly the same way • express my view about belief in Allah.
Level 6	• use religious and philosophical vocabulary to explore belief in Allah • use some of the Arabic words for key Islamic beliefs and actions • consider the challenges for a Muslim of declaring Shahadah and then learning to live by the Five Pillars • use reasoning and examples to show whether practice is as important as belief and the value of good intentions.

Ready for more?

When you have completed this task, you can also work on your skills for Levels 6 and 7, and perhaps even higher. This is an extension task.

'Children should not follow rituals until they are old enough to know their meaning.' Do you agree with this statement? What are your reasons?

- Reflect on the above statement and gather information from throughout Chapter 1, and from the media, to inform a short essay.
- To achieve a high level, you will need to justify your arguments by referring to specific teachings of Islam, and relevant examples from life and from the media.
- You should show that you have thought about this critically and considered the challenges to both children and parents.

Where do Islamic Beliefs Come From?
2.1 Special Feature
And that's Final! The Qur'an

Learning Objectives

In this unit you will:

- examine the Islamic belief that the Qur'an was revealed to the Prophet Muhammad
- explain why and how Muslims try to live by the Qur'an
- reflect on what your most trusted source of advice is.

Starters

- What is your favourite book or film, and why?

Muslims believe that their holy text, the Qur'an, was revealed by Allah to the Prophet Muhammad (see Unit 2.2). Mr Atcha lives in Bolton and explains that, throughout history, Allah had told people how to behave by using 'prophets or messengers'. He says that Muslims believe there are four holy books, including the **Gospels**, but that people did not listen to the messages in the earlier books. Therefore, 'Allah made a promise that the Qur'an was going to be the last book.'

'This is the book; it contains true guidance that is not to be doubted. It will guide all those who fear God.'
The Qur'an 2:2

The Qur'an has 114 chapters (called Surahs), which are made up of verses (called Ayahs).

Many Muslims believe that every Ramadan the Prophet was called upon to recite the whole Qur'an in the presence of angel Jibril. This was to ensure that nothing had been changed from the original **revelation**.

The Qur'an was not written down in the order it was revealed. Because of this, Muslims try to understand the background to the verses and why they were revealed.

a Muslims treat the Qur'an, their holy text, with a great deal of respect.

Muslims use the Qur'an to learn how to behave and to help them get a greater perspective on their lives.

Sarrah Yassin lives in Newport, and says that her family read the Qur'an 'a lot during Ramadan', and that they 'use it during prayers as well'. Many Muslims try to read from the Qur'an every day, and some even try to learn it by heart.

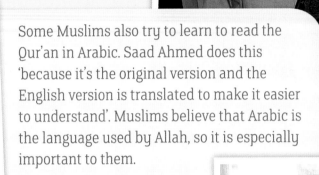

Some Muslims also try to learn to read the Qur'an in Arabic. Saad Ahmed does this 'because it's the original version and the English version is translated to make it easier to understand'. Muslims believe that Arabic is the language used by Allah, so it is especially important to them.

Saad's sister, Rahaf Ahmed, says that reading the Qur'an has a really positive impact on her emotions: 'I read the Qur'an at night, and I wake up happy.'

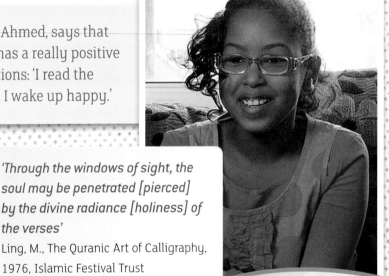

Useful Words

Gospels The four books at the start of the New Testament in the Bible
Revelation Revealing or showing communication from Allah

'Through the windows of sight, the soul may be penetrated [pierced] by the divine radiance [holiness] of the verses'

Ling, M., The Quranic Art of Calligraphy, 1976, Islamic Festival Trust

Reflection

Who or what source do you turn to for good advice? Why?

Activities

1. For each of the young people in the case study, write two interesting questions to ask them about how and why they read the Qur'an.

2. Read the Qur'an quotation on the left page and think about the claim that the Qur'an is 'not to be doubted'. What impact would this have on a Muslim reading it? Discuss with a partner.

3. Imagine that Ling (from the quotation above) is having a discussion with someone who believes that the Qur'an is just a book like any other. Write a dialogue for the conversation that might take place, using the information from this unit.

Learning Objectives

In this unit you will:

- analyse what it means to be a prophet
- evaluate the Islamic belief that Muhammad is the final Prophet of Islam
- reflect on what it is that makes a person trustworthy.

Starter

- If you had to trust one person with an extremely important task, who would it be and why? Discuss with a partner the kinds of tasks you would entrust to different people.

Muslims believe that a Prophet is a messenger sent from Allah to tell them how Allah wants them to behave. Prophets often challenged the world they lived in, or provided encouragement for the people. Muslims believe that many Prophets brought revelations from Allah before Muhammad did.

The **Abrahamic faiths** are Judaism, Christianity and Islam. Three key Jewish and Christian figures are also familiar to Muslims: Nuh (Noah), Ibrahim (Abraham) and Musa (Moses). Muslims refer to these people as Prophets, and believe they taught the message of Islam – to find peace in your life through submission to the one Creator, Allah. Many Muslims have special respect for Isa (Jesus), who they also believe was a Prophet, but they do not agree with Christians that he was the Son of God.

> 'We send the messengers only to give good news and to warn: so those who believe and mend [their lives] – upon them shall be no fear, nor shall they grieve.'
>
> The Qur'an 6:48

? What sort of 'good news' or 'warnings' might a prophet in modern times give to people today?

? Is there anything that you already know about Noah, Moses or Abraham? Make notes in pairs or threes.

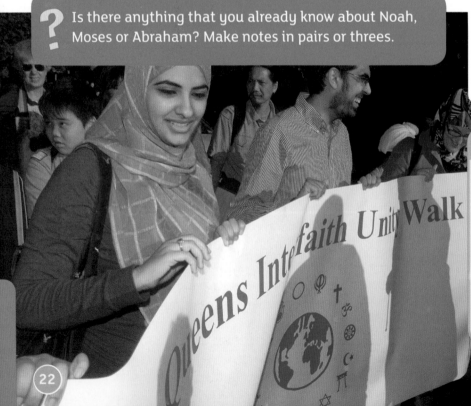

a An inter-faith walk. Although they are very different, Abrahamic faiths do share some key similarities.

Useful Words

Abrahamic faiths Those faiths (Islam, Judaism and Christianity) that acknowledge Abraham as a common origin

Idol worship The worship of statues, or things that are not God

Polytheism Belief in more than one God

Muslims believe that the Prophet Muhammad, a human being, was the last in a long line of Prophets sent to guide people. Muhammad lived in Arabia at a time when it was very dangerous. People were nomadic – meaning they travelled around, rather than settling in one place. There was often fighting and dishonesty, because areas were run by powerful tribal leaders who were often in conflict.

Because many Arabian tribes practised **polytheism** and **idol worship**, one of Muhammad's aims was to teach people that there was only one God – Allah. The Qur'an is believed by Muslims to be the direct Word of Allah. Muslims believe that once the Qur'an was given to humanity, and interpreted through the actions of Muhammad, there was no need for further prophets because Allah had given humanity His word directly.

> '*By the glorious light of morning and by the stillness of night – your Lord, has never forsaken you, and He is not angry with you. Be certain – your future will be better for you than your past, and in the end God will be kind to you and will be satisfied. Did He not find you an orphan, and give you a home? Did He not find you lost and wandering, and showed you the way? Did He not find you in great need, and took care of you? As for you, therefore,* never wrong the orphans, nor turn away those that ask your help; spread and increase your Lord's blessings*'
>
> The Qur'an 93:1–11

b Muhammad's life contained both encouragements and challenges.

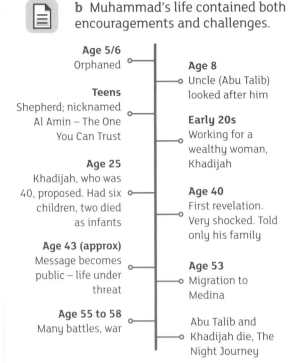

Age 5/6 Orphaned

Age 8 Uncle (Abu Talib) looked after him

Teens Shepherd; nicknamed Al Amin – The One You Can Trust

Early 20s Working for a wealthy woman, Khadijah

Age 25 Khadijah, who was 40, proposed. Had six children, two died as infants

Age 40 First revelation. Very shocked. Told only his family

Age 43 (approx) Message becomes public – life under threat

Age 53 Migration to Medina

Age 55 to 58 Many battles, war

Abu Talib and Khadijah die, The Night Journey

Reflection

How would you feel if you were entrusted with the kind of responsibility that was given to Muhammad?

c Muhammad was sometimes daunted by the great responsibility that had been placed upon him. This famous quotation from the Qur'an is believed by Muslims to have been sent by Allah to reassure him. The brown words show how Muslims believe Allah (referred to as Lord) will look after them. The blue words summarize the kind of role model that the Prophet Muhammad is for Muslims.

Activities

1. Why do you think Muhammad is regarded as the last Prophet by Muslims? Using the information on this spread, suggest an answer to this question.

2. Imagine that you have been asked to introduce Muhammad as a speaker in an assembly. What would you say? Write or record your speech.

3. Look at the above passage from the Qur'an.
   a Name five things that the passage tells Muslims about the nature of Allah.
   b Write three interesting questions that you would ask Muhammad if you could.

Learning Objectives

In this unit you will:

- examine the ups and downs of Muhammad's life
- explore the story of **The Night Journey**, and respond to it philosophically
- consider what helps people during difficult times.

Starters

- Look at the photo on this page and read the quotation. If you felt that life had got you down, what would help you to get back on your feet?

When scholars try to understand the meaning of the Qur'an, and how it should be applied to life today, they look at what was happening when it was revealed. Prophet Muhammad's life had many ups and downs, but Muslims believe that many of the Qur'anic verses supported him when he was struggling with a dilemma in his life, or wondering how to lead the early Muslims.

Muslims believe that in all of these hard times the Prophet Muhammad did not give up, and he still inspires many Muslims who struggle today.

a Muhammad Ali, the famous world champion boxer, was a Muslim.

'Inside of a ring or out, ain't nothing wrong with going down. It's staying down that's wrong.'

b

Challenges	MUHAMMAD	Encouragements
• His loved ones died – his uncle and protector Abu Talib, and his wife Khadijah • He faced **persecution**, e.g. people laid thorns where he walked • He was mocked and stoned • Some tribes, e.g. the **Quraysh**, thought that he was mad	**?** What does it mean that the chosen prophet of Allah went through so many hard times? Think of other key religious figures you have studied – do any of them suffer? Why?	• The support of Muhammad's loved ones • The revelation of the Qur'an • The experience of The Night Journey • The continued respect he has received for both his words and his actions to this day

The Prophet Muhammad's experience of Allah in The Night Journey reminds Muslims that at the centre of their lives is a spiritual journey towards Allah, guided by the Qur'an and the actions of the previous Prophets. It motivated Muhammad at one of the worst times of his life to continue leading people to Islam.

c The Night Journey

Muhammad was sleeping near the Ka'bah when the angel Jibril (Gabriel) shook him awake and took him on a strange horse-like creature with wings, named al-Buraq – the Lightening. He was taken through the seven heavens and shown paradise and hell. In each heaven he met and spoke to earlier prophets – Aaron, Musa (Moses), Ibrahim (Abraham) and Isa (Jesus). He was surprised to find he looked like Ibrahim. Musa told Muhammad that five times a day was the right number of times to pray.

Gradually they approached the highest heaven and the throne of God where Muhammad became aware of a pure, brilliant light which they could not approach.
He felt overwhelming peace and blessings, and his thoughts and feelings disappeared.

Muhammad was returned to earth. The place where he had been lying was still warm and a cup he had tipped over was still emptying. It was all over in a flash.

Reflection

What is the most difficult thing you have ever had to do? Where did you get your strength from? How did it feel?

Activities

1 In pairs or threes, choose one of the following philosophical questions and discuss it in light of the Night Journey story.

  a Does it matter whether this story was a dream or an event that really happened?

  b Do you think Muhammad needed to experience Allah directly?

  c What would be the impact of seeing heaven and hell?

2 Reflect on the impact that The Night Journey would have had on Muhammad, having experienced so much hardship beforehand. How might it have changed him? Express your thoughts by writing the next section of the story – entitled 'What happened when Muhammad returned'.

3 a What does 'spiritual journey' mean? Try to write a definition.

  b In what ways could The Night Journey be considered a spiritual journey?

2.4 Rules, Rules! How do Muslims Know How to Live?

Learning Objectives

In this unit you will:

- examine the ways Muslims decide on the right way to live
- explore and evaluate the main sources of guidance for Muslims
- reflect on the different things that influence you.

Starter

- What are the three most important sources of guidance in your life? In pairs, evaluate their reliability on a scale, where 1 is 'not very reliable' and 10 is 'I would trust this no matter what'. Give reasons.

Muslims believe that, through the Qur'an, Allah has shown them how they should live. Some of the information in the Qur'an is in the form of clear laws. For example, it teaches that Muslims should pray five times a day.

Sometimes the Qur'an gives more general guidance, and in those cases many Muslims will think about what specific actions the Prophet Muhammad took or the advice he gave.

As well as this, scholars have established Islamic laws based on their understanding of the Qur'an and teachings of the Prophet Muhammad, and some Muslims will also keep these in mind.

Useful Words

Hadith The collected sayings of the Prophet Muhammad
Shari'ah Islamic law derived by scholars from the Qur'an, Sunnah and Hadith
Sunnah Actions and teaching of the Prophet Muhammad

Possible sources of authority for Muslims

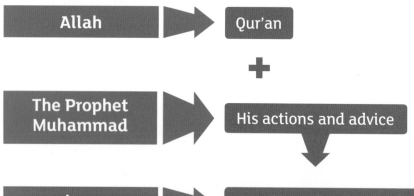

Allah ➡ Qur'an

➕

The Prophet Muhammad ➡ His actions and advice

The collection of information about what actions the Prophet Muhammad took are called **Sunnah**. The advice he gave is all recorded in a collection of sayings called **Hadith**.

Law ➡ Teachings from scholars based on the Qur'an and the life of the Prophet

The law is known by Muslims as **Shari'ah** law.

a The Qur'an, plus the Sunnah and Hadith, is used by scholars to create Shari'ah law.

> 'Hearing and obeying authority are a duty upon the Muslim, whether he likes the orders or not, as long as he is not ordered to disobey Allah: if he is ordered to disobey Allah, then there is neither hearing nor obeying.'
>
> Hadith 3664

b Mo Farah, a famous Muslim athlete, won two gold medals for Britain in the London 2012 Olympic Games. After his victory, he bowed down to thank Allah.

? Try to sum up what this quotation from the Hadith is saying in three bullet points. Discuss with a partner what laws you would obey, even if you didn't like them.

Muslims are expected to obey the laws of the country in which they live. Some countries live under Shari'ah law. In Britain, Muslims do not live under Shari'ah law, but many British laws are supported in the Qur'an. For example, stealing and murder are forbidden.

Sometimes the law of the country prevents Muslims from following their faith in the way they would if they were elsewhere. For example, noise pollution laws in Britain prevent mosques from calling the adhan at prayer time, while in some other countries everyone in the town can hear the call to prayer.

Reflection

Do you consider yourself to be good at following rules? Why or why not?

Activities

1 Look at the Ten Commandments in the Bible (Exodus 20:1–17), which are the basic rules for living for both Jews and Christians, supported in the Qur'an. Do you think they provide a good basis for laws to live by in the twenty-first century? What would you add and what would you take away, and why?

2 Debate – 'When it comes to rules, a book is more reliable than a person'. In pairs, one of you should write down arguments for this statement, and the other should write down arguments against it. Discuss your responses, noting down any good arguments your partner makes.

3 Imagine that a British Muslim is phoning in to a radio station to express their feelings about the noise pollution law. Using the information in this unit, write a script for the conversation between the Muslim and someone giving them advice on what to do.

Learning Objectives

In this unit you will:

- develop an understanding about why and how Muslims believe they are connected to all other Muslims
- explore and explain the concept of **jama'ah** and **ummah**
- reflect upon school as a community.

Starter

- It is sometimes said of relationships that 'blood is thicker than water'. What does that mean? Do you agree?

From the start of Islamic history, the followers of the Prophet Muhammad needed to work together as a community, because they often faced hardship and persecution. In 622 ce, the Prophet's life was threatened and his followers were almost starved in Makkah, because no one would trade with them.

Some people from a town called Yathrib heard the Prophet Muhammad speaking and invited him to be their advisor and to set up his community there. He and his followers migrated to Yathrib in 622 ce, and this became the start of the Islamic community. The city was renamed al-Madinah and the Islamic calendar starts from this date.

Useful Words

Jama'ah Local mosque community of Muslims
Khutbah Sermon at Friday prayers
Ummah Worldwide community of Muslims

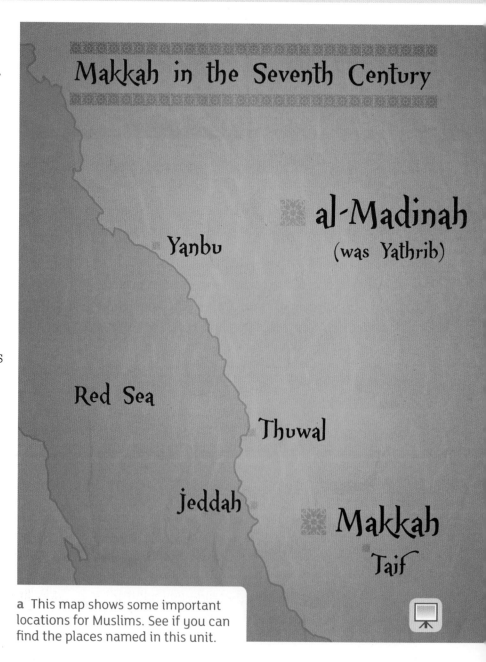

Makkah in the Seventh Century

Yanbu

al-Madinah
(was Yathrib)

Red Sea

Thuwal

Jeddah

Makkah

Taif

a This map shows some important locations for Muslims. See if you can find the places named in this unit.

Since the Prophet encouraged his followers to regard each other as brothers and sisters, the jama'ah (Muslim community) all consider themselves equal in the mosque. The jama'ah must all meet for Friday prayers and hear the **khutbah** and collect zakah, as well as providing an Islamic education for children.

As a community, the jama'ah will offer to help settle any arguments, to support each other in any way possible, and to make sure that no member of the community is in difficulty or hardship without help being offered. Muslims also use the word ummah to describe the worldwide community of Muslims, and try to care for all Muslims – no matter where they are.

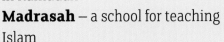

Kitchen – for breaking fast in Ramadan
Madrasah – a school for teaching Islam
Meeting room – for social gatherings, weddings, etc.
Shop – for selling Islamic artefacts
Morgue – where the dead are prepared for burial

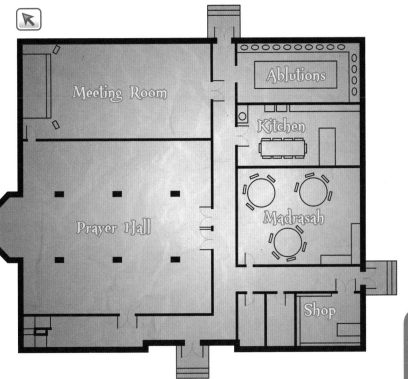

Meeting Room

Ablutions

Kitchen

Prayer Hall

Madrasah

Shop

Morgue

b The many roles performed by a mosque and its community.

Reflection

What does your school do to create the feeling of community? What other ways of improving this aspect of your school can you suggest?

? As well as being their place of worship, the mosque is a community centre that supports local Muslims. Which activity described above do you think provides the best support for the community?

Activities

1. In pairs, make a poster for display in a mosque to encourage Muslims to keep being part of the Islamic community. Use the information in this unit.

2. Write a brief, including sketches if you like, for an architect who wants to build a new mosque – what features would you include and why?

3. 'Muslim brothers and sisters are not as important as real siblings.' How might a Muslim respond to this? Consider arguments for and against.

Objectives

- Investigate and analyse the key ideas that arise from the story of The Night Journey.

- Show that you understand that for Muslims, everything leads back to the Qur'an, because they consider it to be the Word of Allah.

- Express your views about the significance of The Night Journey being either real or a dream.

Task

Produce a piece of artwork, or a storyboard, to show The Night Journey. See how many ideas you can get into your work.

a **Prepare**: Reread the section about The Night Journey in Unit 2.3, and list the key ideas. There are at least ten, plus ideas arising from the difficult times that the Prophet Muhammad was facing before The Night Journey.

b **Produce**: Create your artwork. **Remember**: Muslims do not draw pictures of the Prophet Muhammad and other people, especially not Allah.

c **Evaluate**: Create a display of pictures. The whole class should then use a checklist of ideas to evaluate all of the pictures and decide which one includes the most ideas and presents them in the best way.

a

A bit of guidance...

This task allows you to showcase, in particular, your skills of investigation, analysis and expression.

The Night Journey is a rich story that contains a lot of ideas. It's possible to include all of them in one picture. Be creative – it can be abstract art or realistic. Just don't draw people or Allah.

Hints and tips

To help you tackle this task, you could do some of the following:

- Establish links between events in The Night Journey and key Islamic beliefs, and think of ways you could make these clear in your work.

- Consider what style of artwork you want to produce and what materials you have available.

Guidance

What level are you aiming at? Have a look at the grid below to see what you need to do to achieve that level. What would you need to do to improve your work?

	I can...
Level 3	• include a few of the key ideas from The Night Journey, such as the winged horse • describe the events in the story.
Level 4	• include some key words as part of my picture/storyboard • make some reference to the difficult times that the Prophet Muhammad was facing.
Level 5	• include most of the main elements of The Night Journey • evaluate whether others have done the same with their pictures • demonstrate understanding of how the story might impact Muslims.
Level 6	• include all of the key elements of The Night Journey • express complex ideas in a creative and symbolic way • help the viewer to decide whether this was a dream or a miracle • evaluate others' work clearly, giving reasons for your views and constructive feedback.

Ready for more?

When you have completed this task, you can also work on your skills for Levels 6 and 7, and perhaps even higher. This is an extension task.

'It does not matter whether The Night Journey was real or a dream, if it supported the Prophet Muhammad at a critical time.'

• Reflect on the above statement and use your understanding from the work you have done to inform a short essay (two or three paragraphs).

• Consider evidence for and against the statement before reaching a conclusion.

• To achieve a high level, you will need to justify your arguments and consider very carefully the difficult times facing the Prophet Muhammad and how The Night Journey provided support.

• Think about the meaning of the story for Muslims today, and whether it's necessary for them to believe that a miracle took place.

Learning Objectives

In this unit you will:

- develop an understanding about why Muslims have set times for prayer
- analyse the significance of prayer in Muslims' lives
- reflect on how you please people you care about.

Starter

- In pairs, create a spider diagram titled: 'Why do people pray?' Include your thoughts, ideas and questions.

The second pillar of Islam is **salah**. Muslims pray five times a day at set times, facing towards **Makkah**. The times are set according to the movement of the sun, not at a fixed time, which means that prayer times change with the seasons. Most of the words of the prayer are the same each time.

Muslims believe that praying is good, because it helps them connect with Allah. Rules were given to the Prophet Muhammad by Allah, during The Night Journey (see Unit 2.3), as the correct number of prayers each day to help people to stay focused on Allah. Many Muslims follow these rules because of 'submission', which means they accept Allah's authority over them.

> 'Prophet Muhammad said, "Do you see that if there were a river at the door of one of you, and he was to bathe in it five times a day, would there be any dirt left upon him?" They replied, "No dirt would be left upon him." He said, "That is the example of the five prayers: Allah erases sins by way of them".'
>
> Hadith 330

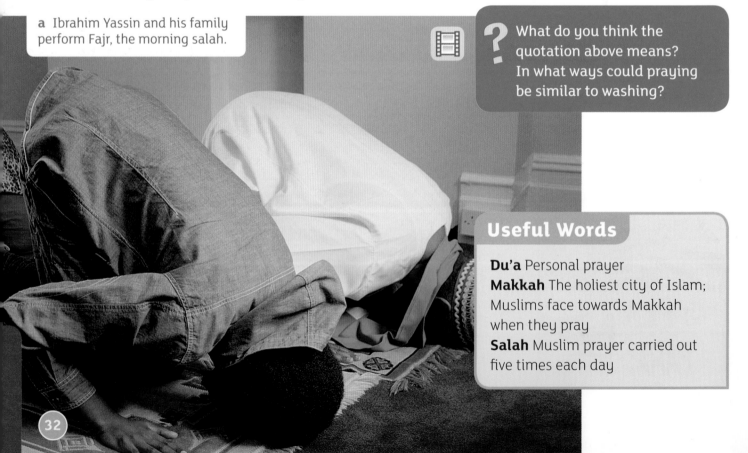

a Ibrahim Yassin and his family perform Fajr, the morning salah.

? What do you think the quotation above means? In what ways could praying be similar to washing?

Useful Words

Du'a Personal prayer

Makkah The holiest city of Islam; Muslims face towards Makkah when they pray

Salah Muslim prayer carried out five times each day

Caps are worn by Muslim men to cover their heads out of respect when praying.

Prayer mats are small carpets that Muslims kneel on to pray. The design often includes arches to point towards Makkah, and sometimes compasses for finding the direction of prayer. Muslims don't leave these mats on the floor between prayers – they are folded tidily and kept clean.

The Qur'an must not be placed on the floor, so it is placed on a stand when reading. Many Qur'an stands are carved with Islamic designs.

Prayer beads are used to help to count the number of prayers when reciting special words or the 99 names of Allah. These can range from little plastic beads to beautiful stones.

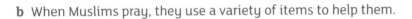

b When Muslims pray, they use a variety of items to help them.

At prayer time, many Muslims will stand on their prayer mats and fold their hands in front of them. Prayer often starts with the person saying the following phrase, which is the first verse in the Qur'an:

Bismillah ir-Rahman ir-Rahim
'In the name of Allah, Most Gracious, Most Merciful'

This verse helps put Muslims in the right state of mind before they praise and thank Allah, and then ask Him for guidance. What do you think it means to pray 'in the name of Allah'?

Muslims also say a personal prayer to Allah called **du'a**, which can be made in their own words and can be done at any time.

? Which prayer aid do you think is the most important? Why?

Reflection

Muslims pray salah because they know that this is what Allah wants. Do you ever give up time to please other people? When and why?

Activities

1 Muslims have two different types of prayer. Using the information in this unit, explore why there are two types in a format of your choice (collage, poem, etc.).

2 What might the advantages and disadvantages be if someone always says the same words and performs the same actions when they pray? Make a list and discuss with a partner.

3 Consider the photo of the Yassin family praying. Explain how Muslims pray in thoughts, word and action.

Learning Objectives

In this unit you will:

- investigate why Muslims believe that giving to charity is essential
- explain the difference between **zakah** and **sadaqah**
- reflect on whether giving time is more important than giving money.

Starter

- How do you feel about sharing what's yours with your friends and family?
- Would you share with a stranger in the same way?

The third pillar of Islam is zakah. Every year, around the festival of **Eid-ul-Fitr**, most Muslims will pay zakah. This requires them to give a percentage of their savings to help the poor and needy. After they have paid all of their bills, many Muslims will donate 2.5% of their annual savings.

Zakah is collected as a kind of tax in some Islamic countries, but in the UK many Muslims pay by donation to a charity – or by placing their zakah in a collection box in the local mosque (where a committee decides how it should be spent). Muslims call each other brother or sister – this reminds them that Allah has made them responsible for each other.

? If you had £1,000 in savings, how much zakah would you pay at 2.5%? Try to work it out in pairs or threes. How would you feel about giving this much money away?

a There are many Muslim charities (such as Muslim Hands and Save an Orphan) that Muslims can choose to donate to.

According to the Qur'an, zakah can be spent on:

- helping the poor and needy ✓
- the daily needs of students of the Qur'an ✓
- supporting converts to Islam ✓
- any action in the cause of Allah. ✓

Specific people at mosques or Muslim charities are given responsibility for making sure that zakah is used properly. They use lists like these to guide them.

Useful Words

Eid-ul-Fitr The celebration at the end of Ramadan, after a month of fasting
Sadaqah Any good deed done for the sake of Allah, rather than selfish reasons
Zakah Payment of 2.5% of annual savings

? Which do you think are the most important things that zakah can be spent on?

Zakah is not the only way in which Muslims give charity. In fact, Muslims are encouraged to give more than just money – they are encouraged to approach life with a generous attitude. While zakah is a compulsory payment, sadaqah is optional, and it may involve Muslims giving their time, talent, money or prayer. Sadaqah can also be small, kind things that they do for people. For Muslims, the important thing about sadaqah is that it encourages them to give freely.

> 'The deeds most loved by Allah are those that are done regularly even though they may be small.'
> Hadith

> 'By no means shall you attain righteousness [being morally right] unless you give of that which you love; and whatever of good you give, Allah knows it well'
> The Qur'an 3:92

? What do you think the second passage means? Why does it say that a person should give what they love?

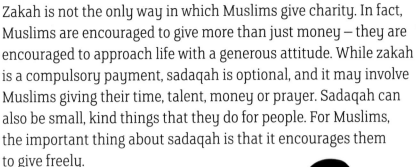

Reflection

'Giving time is more important than giving money.' Do you agree? Why/why not? Give some examples of how giving time could be a form of sadaqah.

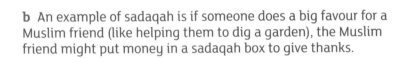

b An example of sadaqah is if someone does a big favour for a Muslim friend (like helping them to dig a garden), the Muslim friend might put money in a sadaqah box to give thanks.

Activities

1 Discuss with a partner: 'Why do you think many Muslims pay the same percentage of their annual savings, rather than everyone having to pay the same amount?'

2 Think about zakah and sadaqah.
   a Write a definition of each type of giving, using no more than 15 words each.
   b Note down the similarities and differences.

c Why do you think Muslims have zakah as well as sadaqah? Write two sentences to explain your reasons.

3 'The government should take care of poor people. It's not for individuals to worry about them.' Write your response to this statement. How might a Muslim respond to this?

Learning Objectives

In this unit you will:

- develop an understanding about why Muslims fast in Ramadan
- evaluate the Islamic view that self-restraint is a valuable skill
- reflect on your own views about how difficult it is to deny ourselves the things we want.

Starter

- What do you do if you're hungry just before dinner? How long can you wait for food?

Sawm is the fourth pillar of Islam and means fasting. From just before dawn until sunset for the 29 or 30 days of the month of Ramadan, Muslims are required to go without food, drink (including water), and some other things. Even after sunset, they should not take too much of these things. They should also try to control emotions such as anger and greed.

As well as adults, all Muslim boys and girls who have reached adolescence must fast during Ramadan. However, some Muslims can choose not to fast during Ramadan (for example, people who are ill, or women who are pregnant). But these people are expected to make up their fast later, when they can.

> '0 you who believe! Fasting is prescribed [told] to you as it was prescribed to those before you that you may learn self-restraint.'
> The Qur'an 2:183

? What reason does this give for fasting? Is it a good reason, in your opinion?

a After sunset, Muslims break their fast, usually by first eating dates, as Muhammad is believed to have broken fast in this way.

Useful Words

Sawm Fasting; going without food or drink from dawn to sunset

Sometimes families wait with great excitement for the start of the month of Ramadan. Islamic months follow the moon's cycle, so this will be when the new moon is first seen – either from their local mosque, or in Makkah, Saudi Arabia. This is announced excitedly on TV and at the mosque.

Muslims try to make sure that they are with family and friends at sunset, when they break fast – usually with water and a few dates, because this is what the Prophet Muhammad did.

> 'Whoever does not give up speaking falsehood and acting upon it, Allah has no need of his fasting in giving up his food and drink'
>
> Hadith 1999

? What does this quotation mean? How does it support Sarrah and Ibrahim's views?

Case Study

Ibrahim and Sarrah Yassin explain why they believe fasting at Ramadan is important.

> It is less about the lack of food and more about the spirituality behind it.

> It's about being at peace with yourself and at peace with everybody else. It is also about remembering the less fortunate, so that we are grateful for what we have.

Reflection

Do you ever find it difficult to be patient? What helps you?

Activities

1. On a piece of paper, write down the words 'fasting', 'starving' and 'dieting'. What are the differences between them? What is similar? Make notes around your words, including the Islamic view.

2. Create a mind-map about the kinds of difficulty a British Muslim might face when fasting.

3. Can you think of other ways to develop self-restraint (e.g. patience, discipline and self-control)? Could you do this for a whole month?

4. Sarrah feels greater compassion for those who are truly starving when she fasts. Do you think it is necessary to experience someone else's problems in order to understand them? Discuss with a partner.

Learning Objectives

In this unit you will:

- explore Hajj as an example of Islamic pilgrimage
- identify the features which make Hajj spiritual
- reflect on times when you consider the meaning of life.

Starter

- Use creative calligraphy to write the name of a place that is important to you. Can others work out how you feel about the place from your design?

The Hajj **pilgrimage** is the fifth pillar of Islam. It is a special journey that many Muslims are required to go on (when they are healthy and can afford it) at least once in their lifetime. However, it is physically demanding and can be expensive. Not everyone can complete Hajj, but many Muslims believe that those who are able to do so should.

'And proclaim to the people the Hajj; they will come to you on foot and on every lean camel; they will come from every distant pass – That they may witness benefits for themselves and mention the name of Allah on known days over what He has provided for them'

The Qur'an 22:27–28

? What reasons does this quotation give Muslims about why they should complete Hajj?

Some things I should do on Hajj:

- State the intention to set my heart on Hajj.
- Put on special clothes.
- Recite 'I obey you, I am at your service'.
- Circle the Ka'bah seven times.
- Travel to Mina, Arafat and al-Madinah to perform the rituals involved, including stoning **Shaytan** and the sacrifice of Eid-ul-Fitr.

a Look at the following to find out where Muslims go on Hajj and what they do. Is there anything that you would like to know more about?

Useful Words

Ka'bah A cube-shaped structure in the centre of the grand mosque in Makkah; it does not contain anything to worship – in fact, Muhammad removed all 'idols' from it

Pilgrimage A special journey with spiritual intention

Shaytan Satan, or the devil

The Ka'bah at Makkah is the holiest place in Islam – many Muslims believe that it was built by Adam and restored by Ibrahim (Abraham) and Isma'il (Ishmael). The Prophet Muhammad and his early followers used to make an annual pilgrimage to Makkah.

Previously, the journey to Makkah was difficult and dangerous, and took many weeks. Now that accommodation and flights to and from Saudi Arabia are readily available, it is easy to forget the difficulties faced by early Muslims that made Hajj an extra special commitment.

Case Study

? This is the Ka'bah at Makkah. Using your five senses to imagine what it might be like, write a poem or diary entry expressing what Muslims might experience as they circle the Ka'bah.

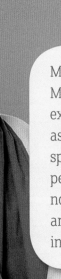

Mr and Mrs Yassin have both completed Hajj. Mr Yassin says that it was a 'wonderful, wonderful experience'. He says that the most challenging aspect is the conditions, because the Qur'an (2:197) specifically states that pilgrims should remain peaceful: 'The hardest bit is being peaceful, not to harm anything, not to get into an argument. There are millions of people in Hajj, so it is difficult to keep peaceful.'

Reflection

What would you do for something you believe in? How could hardship make you stronger?

Activities

1. List five differences between tourist travel and pilgrimage.

2. In pairs or threes, use hot-seating to explore how it might have felt for Mr and Mrs Yassin to remain peaceful amongst the crowds, and to finally reach the Ka'bah.

3. People sometimes say that going to a major sporting event to support your team is like making a pilgrimage. How is it similar and how is it different? Write your answer as an advertisement for a trip to a major sporting event, like the World Cup or the Olympics.

3.5 Are You What You Eat? Halal and Haram Food

Learning Objectives

In this unit you will:

- explain reasons for Islamic food rules
- develop an understanding of halal and haram
- consider the relevance of food rules in modern times.

Starter

- What do you like to eat?
- Do you ever get a craving for anything?

Many Muslims live their whole lives without ever knowing what some popular food and drink items taste like (e.g. pork sausages and bacon, or alcohol). They try to live by certain instructions in the Qur'an that tell them what they can and cannot eat. As well as this, Islam also provides guidance on the right attitude to food – in terms of staying physically and spiritually healthy.

> *'So eat of [meats] on which Allah's name has been pronounced [said], if ye [you] have faith in His signs.'*
> The Qur'an 6:118

Case Study

Mrs Atcha says that, in Islam, foods considered permissible or lawful for Muslims are called halal: 'Halal means that the food has been slaughtered or prepared in a certain way.' She goes on to explain: 'In Islam, whatever we consume has to be not only halal but also tayyib, which means pure.'

When an animal is killed for food in Islam, the halal killing includes a prayer said over the animal to thank Allah for allowing people to eat meat. The way the animal is killed is also designed to make sure that it dies instantly.

Mrs Atcha explains that Muslims are 'not allowed to be cruel to the animals. Not only does it have to be halal but how we process it has to be pure until it gets to our plate'.

Foodstuffs that are considered unlawful or forbidden are called haram (e.g. products from pigs, as well as alcohol).

? What do you think 'pure' means? Discuss with a partner.

Alcohol is considered by many Muslims to be haram, because it changes someone's state of mind and can lead to them doing bad things or being less focused on Allah.

A Sunnah of the Prophet Muhammad also tells Muslims the correct attitude to food. He said that the stomach should be one third for food, one third for water and one third for air (i.e. empty), and that people should leave the table feeling as though they could still eat more.

> **?** What reasons do you think the Prophet Muhammad might have had for saying this?

Case Study

Many Muslims do not drink alcohol.

'If a restaurant were to serve alcohol we would be less likely to choose to go there.'

Reflection

Do you ever think about what you are eating and where it comes from?

Activities

1. Using the information from this unit, design a fridge magnet which reminds Muslims about the attitude they should have towards food. Justify your design and information choices.

2. Research and make a list of food and drink items considered halal or haram for Muslims. In a different colour, add in any relevant situations or jobs that Muslims might need to avoid.

3. 'Food rules make no sense in modern times.' Discuss, justifying your points of view.

4. Choose either Mrs Atcha or the Prophet Muhammad and make a list of interesting questions to ask them about what it means to be physically and spiritually healthy.

3.6 What do You See When You Look at Me? Islamic Dress

Learning Objectives

In this unit you will:

- develop an understanding about and explain why some Muslims dress the way they do
- analyse what affects the way people dress
- reflect on and discuss whether it matters how we dress.

Starter

- What do your clothes say about you?
- Where in your life are there dress code expectations?

People often think that they can recognize Muslims by the way they dress. There are some stereotypical ideas about Islamic dress, but – as almost 1 in 4 people on the planet is Muslim – there are in fact many different variations in dress, depending on climate, local culture and belief.

> '0 ye Children of Adam! We have bestowed raiment [clothing] upon you to cover your shame, as well as to be an adornment [decoration] to you. But the raiment of righteousness, that is the best…'
> The Qur'an 7:26

? What does the Qur'an say the purpose of clothing is? What do you think the 'raiment of **righteousness**' is?

A niqab is a full-face covering worn by some Muslim women.

A hijab is a Muslim woman's head, hair and chest covering.

Some Muslims choose not to wear Islamic clothing.

Mosque clothes are traditional clothes worn by some Muslim men to go to the mosque.

? In the Qur'an, Muslim men and women are required to dress modestly. Can you explain '**modesty**' in your own words?

Useful Words

Modesty Decency of behaviour, speech and dress
Righteousness Being moral or acting properly

It is commonly thought that Muslim women have to cover their hair with a hijab whenever they are in public, but many Muslims believe that – because covering should be an outward sign of their 'inner' attitude – this is a choice that every woman should make for herself.

Case Study

Mrs Atcha chooses to wear the hijab: 'My mum wore it and it was something I was expected to do at 14 and that's what I did. But, as I became older, I wore it as my own decision.' She does it to be 'modest', to 'humble' herself, and to 'sacrifice' an aspect of her beauty.

When asked whether she would expect her daughter to wear the hijab, Mrs Atcha said: 'I'd like for her to choose and understand why she chooses to. If she chooses not to, I would expect her to dress modestly.'

Yasmin is a British Muslim who chooses not to wear any kind of Islamic clothing: 'My faith is really important to me, but I don't believe I need to wear a hijab. I don't think it's right to flaunt my body, but neither do I think that I should hide myself away, when beauty is a gift from Allah.'

Reflection

Do you ever make judgements about people based on their clothing? When and why?

Activities

1. For Mrs Atcha and Yasmin, write three interesting questions that you would ask each of them. With a partner, suggest possible answers to each other's questions.

2. Is it better to do something because you believe it is right or because you're told to?

3. Design clothing for a young British Muslim (male or female) who chooses not to wear Islamic clothing, but who wants to dress modestly. Make notes on your design explaining how modesty might be interpreted in British culture.

Learning Objectives

In this unit you will:

- examine how and why Muslims celebrate two main Eid festivals
- identify key Islamic beliefs shown by the story of **Eid-ul-Adha**
- evaluate and explain reasons for remembering historical events.

Starter

- Discuss in pairs your favourite kind of party. Note down all the details of your ideal celebration.

The Arabic word 'Eid' means celebration. Muslims love to party at festival time, and they have two big celebrations each year, Eid-ul-Adha and **Eid-ul-Fitr**.

Eid-ul-Adha means 'Festival of sacrifice'. It reminds Muslims of when the Prophet Ibrahim was asked by Allah to sacrifice his son, but was provided with an animal to sacrifice once he had shown his devotion to Allah. Muslims celebrate this story because it reminds them to develop obedience and trust, which are key to their relationship with Allah. Eid-ul-Adha comes at the end of Hajj, which makes it a very special time because it links Muslims to their history and their most sacred place. During their visit to Mina, many Muslims will sacrifice an animal and share it out amongst the poor.

In Britain, it is usual for Muslims to pay for an animal to be given to the poor in another country via a worldwide charity. This meat is called **qurbani**. During these festivals, many Muslims will also offer special prayers at the mosque.

? Many Muslims sacrifice an animal during Eid-ul-Adha to symbolize the Prophet Ibrahim's sacrifice of a ram. What do you think 'sacrifice' means in this context? Why do you think it happens?

a British Muslims celebrating during an Eid festival.

Useful Words

Eid-ul-Adha Festival of sacrifice
Eid-ul-Fitr Festival of breaking the fast
Qurbani The meat of animals sacrificed at Eid-ul-Adha that are shared with family and the poor

Case Study

Eid-ul-Fitr means 'Festival of breaking the fast', and is a big celebration after the end of Ramadan (the Islamic month of fasting and prayer). Sarrah Yassin says that during this festival, Muslims 'gather as a community' at the mosque. They 'have food, wear new clothes, and the imam says a prayer and gives a speech on how to live in the way of the Prophet Muhammad'. She adds that people 'hug each other after the prayer to say sorry about things – it's almost like a fresh start'.

After the visit to the mosque, families get together. People will even travel far across the country to be together.

Sarrah's brother, Ibrahim, describes how Eid-ul-Fitr has changed for him over time:

When I was younger, it was all meeting friends and getting together and having fun and sweets and presents – not too different from how Christmas is for Christians.

As I got older I started to learn the meaning behind Eid – and the spiritual aspects – and it became more of an adult thing. The presents are just the outer showing of the goodness inside. Eid-ul-Fitr can be quite sad, because it's the closing of Ramadan, which is a spiritual time.

Reflection

How is Eid-ul-Fitr similar to and different from celebrations that you have been involved in?

Activities

1. Muslims celebrate Eid-ul-Adha to remind themselves of the importance of the Prophet Ibrahim's obedience. In what ways do you try to learn from events in your past? How does it impact on your life?

2. Write a diary entry for either Ibrahim or Sarrah Yassin about their experiences of Eid-ul-Fitr, including details of the festival and how it feels to celebrate it.

3. 'Festivals are just a good excuse for a party, they're not spiritually significant.' How would you respond to this? How would a Muslim respond to you?

Chapter 3 Assessment
Belonging to the Islamic Faith

Objectives

- Demonstrate that you know how being a Muslim affects day to day life and community events.
- Demonstrate empathy with Muslims trying to follow the rules of Islam.

Task

Draw on your learning about the Five Pillars, festivals and the Islamic community to plan an Eid party for an Islamic youth group. Be prepared to present your plan to the mosque committee for approval.

a   Prepare: In groups of three or four, decide what is important to a Muslim about Ramadan and Eid. Then think about when and where you will hold the party, what food you will serve and when. Finally, consider what the party dress code is, and how you will involve the community.

b   Plan: Use your research to plan all aspects of the party. Decide how you will persuade people to help you get the party ready.

c   Evaluate: Each group should vote on which of the planned parties they would prefer to attend, and explain why.

a

A bit of guidance...

This task will allow you to show your skills of synthesis (pulling together different ideas), empathy, and application (applying your knowledge).

Start by thinking about all the topics raised in section (a) above, and then combine your group's knowledge to make decisions. Identify things that are compulsory in Islam and build them into your plan.

Hints and tips

To help you tackle this task, you could do some of the following:

- Use examples from the news, TV, *Islam Kerboodle* video clips and 'real life' to support your views. For example, images of Eid parties, etc.
- Allocate responsibilities for researching different aspects within your group, e.g. food, clothing, organization and practical matters, artwork for posters, etc. Use everybody's abilities and work to their strengths.

Guidance

What level are you aiming at? Have a look at the grid below to see what you need to do to achieve that level. What would you need to do to improve your work?

	I can ...
Level 3	• say why Muslims have a party at Eid • describe some areas of life which may need to be considered when planning an event for Muslims, e.g. food and clothes.
Level 4	• use religious words to refer to key ideas in Islam • refer to the Five Pillars in the party plan and show understanding of how they impact the lives of Muslims
Level 5	• plan activities for Muslims that demonstrate a good knowledge of Islam • explain the differences between religious and non-religious parties • express clearly to others why certain elements have been included in the plan with reference to Islam
Level 6	• explain the importance of Ramadan in the lives of Muslims and say which of the Five Pillars should be observed before someone attends a party • demonstrate that a range of Islamic perspectives have been evaluated and the plan allows for different practices • evaluate the work of other groups, providing constructive feedback.

Ready for more?

When you have completed this task, you can also work on your skills for Levels 6 and 7, and perhaps even higher. This is an extension task.

Write a khutbah for Ramadan. A khutbah is a speech given by a religious leader in the mosque at prayers. It contains guidance to Muslims about how to live their lives. Many Muslims attend Eid prayers at the mosque before attending an Eid party.

• To achieve a high level, you will need to use a wide religious and philosophical vocabulary, and to present a coherent understanding that reflects your views about how issues related to Ramadan should be dealt with by Muslims in their everyday lives.

• You should include your personal response and show that you understand the challenges of what you're preaching.

Learning Objectives

In this unit you will:

- examine why life after death is important for Muslims
- identify how Islamic belief in an afterlife influences their actions
- reflect on what you think is the purpose of life.

Many Muslims believe that this life is temporary, and is merely a preparation for Akhirah – eternal life. Muslims believe in heaven (which is a good place) and hell (which is a terrible place). They also believe that there are many things beyond human understanding. Muslims try to remain aware that everything works in the way that Allah wants it, and that they will be tested with challenges to overcome if they want to get to heaven.

Case Study

Ibrahim Yassin believes the 'key to getting into heaven' is doing good deeds to obtain Allah's mercy: 'Because Allah loves us, he wouldn't want to chuck us into hell for small things. It's not just about doing a few very good deeds, but about doing little things all the time – helping someone here or removing an obstacle from someone's path.'

Ibrahim's sister, Sarrah, agrees that leading a peaceful life is important: 'If there was no life after death, I'd still be happy, because I'd know I lived life peacefully and in harmony with everyone else.' Sarrah believes that 'our world is controlled by the imperfect decisions of people today, but the afterlife is controlled by Allah's mercy and grace'.

? Reflect on Ibrahim and Sarrah's beliefs about good deeds and the afterlife. Do you think their beliefs make them more likely to do good deeds than someone who does not believe in life after death? Why or why not?

Muslims believe that there are different parts to people.

b An Islamic artwork of heaven including calligraphy

a

> Muslims believe that the physical body must be kept healthy as it houses the spirit which Allah breathes into humans, often called the soul.

> The soul is sometimes known as rouh. It enters the body when it is still in its mother's womb and spends the short time on earth until death. Then it will wait in the grave until judgement day, before being given back its body to go to heaven or hell. It cannot be seen and is 'beyond the physical', connected to God.

> Another word – nafs – is used to describe the soul once it has entered the body. At this point, the soul can be described as someone's persona — the non-physical part of us that helps us to make choices.

? What do you think of the explanation in the boxes above? Would you change anything?

Reflection

What do you think happens when we die? What factors might have influenced your thoughts?

Activities

1 In pairs, hot-seat Sarrah Yassin to explore why she thinks human decisions are not perfect, and then Ibrahim Yassin to explore what it feels like to continually do small good deeds. What other questions would you ask them?

2 Design your own version of the body diagram on this page, based on the different aspects you think make up a human. Include labels with reasons for your choices, and also include (where relevant) your comments on how it compares with the Islamic viewpoint.

3 Look at the image on this page, which shows a depiction of heaven.
  a Does this image show that heaven is 'controlled by Allah's mercy and grace', as Sarrah says? Why or why not?
  b Produce a piece of artwork showing your own idea of heaven or hell.

Learning Objectives

In this unit you will:

- examine Islamic attitudes to death and bereavement
- explain the concept of shirk
- reflect on whether belief in an afterlife comforts people facing death.

Many Muslims believe that two angels are always on their shoulders – the right-hand one recording any good deeds, and the left-hand one recording any bad deeds. When they say 'as-salamu alaykum wa rahmatullah', and turn their heads to the right and left at the end of prayers, they believe that they are greeting these angels.

Muslims believe that they will be judged after death based on the balance of all of their actions in life. They also believe that their intentions matter – good acts can be done with the wrong intention (such as giving money to charity but seeking praise for your generosity) and bad acts with a good intention (such as someone who is too tired to read the Qur'an one day because they are working overtime to support their family).

> 'Three things follow the funeral procession of a dead man: the members of his family, his wealth and his good deeds. Two of them come back: his family and his wealth; and his deeds alone are left with him'
>
> Hadith 42: 1999

The worst sin is to believe in something other than Allah at the time of death, or saying that Allah has an equal. This is called shirk. Muslims believe that only Allah knows when someone will die – and that death can arrive at any time – so they try to stay constantly aware of Allah.

? Create a piece of work that explores the idea put forward in the quotation in a format of your choice.

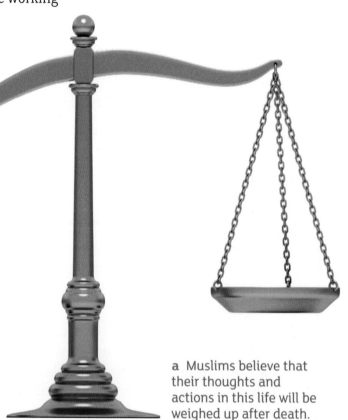

a Muslims believe that their thoughts and actions in this life will be weighed up after death.

Some Muslims say that this life is really spent asleep, and people are only truly awake after they die – when the spirit has answered its call to Allah. Muslims are naturally sad about the loss of loved ones, but they are encouraged not to become overwhelmed with grief because they believe that Allah knows what is best for everyone in the end.

? Which Islamic beliefs are reflected in how Muslims act when someone dies?

 What happens when a Muslim dies?

The dead body is washed and covered with white sheets, before being buried facing Makkah.

An angel is believed to come down from heaven to take the soul away.

The deceased person is often kept in a special place at the mosque, called a morgue.

The funeral usually takes place within 24 hours of death. It is a duty on the local jama'ah to attend the funeral (men only), and a special prayer is said.

Friends visit the bereaved family to pay their respects and bring food. They spend a lot of time reading the Qur'an in the 40 days after death.

b

Reflection

How does the idea of death make you feel? What would bring you comfort?

Activities

1 **a** Think about the last two days. Draw some old-fashioned weighing scales and list all of your good deeds on the right and all of your bad deeds on the left. What do you think of your decisions? Do your intentions change things?

b Make a list of advice to help a Muslim keep the angel on the right shoulder busy and give the angel on the left shoulder less to do.

2 Why does intention matter? Isn't it enough to do the right thing no matter what your reasons are?

Learning Objectives

In this unit you will:

- analyse the belief held by some Muslims that life is a test
- identify and explore the two meanings of jihad
- reflect on what you do when you face difficulty.

Starter

- Talk to a partner about a time when you were pushed to the limit. In your pairs, discuss both of your situations and evaluate the self-control you both showed.

Case Study

Many Muslims believe that life is a test. They believe that specific tests are set by Allah to help them develop qualities they lack. Because of this, they accept that sometimes life is a struggle – but they look forward to becoming more and more like the kind of person Allah describes in the Qur'an.

Rahaf Ahmed says that living far away from her family and friends feels like a test, 'because most of my family live in Africa'. She says 'it's hard being away from them and not talking to them every day, like other families do'. Many Muslims believe that tests like this develop patience and courage in a person.

Rahaf's brother, Saad, says that a personal struggle for him is 'exams, and not having time to do other things like go out with friends'. However, he thinks that being 'patient in hard times' gives him hope. He says that it's possible to know when a person has passed a test, because they 'keep believing in Allah, and don't give up on Him'.

? Rahaf and Saad believe that life is a test. What impact does this belief have on them?

Surveys of Muslim populations across the world show jihad is understood to mean different things. Jihad means the inner spiritual struggle, the duty to strive in the way of God against sin. Saad and Rahaf describe this 'greater jihad' as a way in which Allah develops good qualities within them. This might mean being just or honest.

Jihad is the struggle to make a good living and so contribute to a good society. To strive for a good society might include a struggle or protest against persecution and oppression. For some jihad can be a defence of the faith, even using violence. However, this is controversial because violent extremists use jihad to justify things that seem to go against Islam.

? Look carefully at the two photographs and make a note of your responses. Discuss your feelings with a partner and identify three questions you'd like to ask about the photos. Share and discuss in a small group. What further information is needed to help you answer the questions?

a Muslims peacefully protesting against acts of terror.

b A London bus destroyed by a suicide bomber on 7 July 2005, a day when a series of similar attacks left 52 civilians dead.

Activities

1 Interview your partner about something they learned from a challenging situation.

2 In pairs, role-play or write down a conversation between a young Muslim who is facing a personal struggle and someone who is giving them advice on how they should approach it.

3 What kind things do/might Rahaf and Saad find to be a challenge, and what qualities do you think they develop as a result of this 'jihad'?

4 Look at the two photos (a and b). One shows Scottish Muslims protesting against terrorism and the other an act of terror carried out by someone who thought they were doing the right thing. If you could write a letter to send back to each, to arrive the day before these photos were taken, what would you write? Think about the qualities you think we should encourage in people.

Reflection

Reflect on the personal struggles faced by Rahaf and Saad. What are the similar challenges you might face in your own daily life?

Learning Objectives

In this unit you will:

- examine further the idea that for Muslims, life is a test
- evaluate the idea that the acceptance of life as a test makes suffering easier to bear
- consider whether we should accept suffering as part of life.

People suffer because of events like natural disasters, and also because of things that other people do. Seeing images like the one on this page can be upsetting, and lead many people to ask: 'Why does this happen?'

In times of suffering, many Muslims take comfort from the idea that everyone will be judged by Allah on everything that they do in their lives. Islam sets out harsh punishments for people who commit acts that make others suffer, such as murder.

Muslims often say: 'Everything happens for a reason', because they believe that Allah has a plan for everyone. When something bad happens, it can cause many people to question what kind of god would allow it, or even whether a god exists. Islam teaches, however, that Muslims should rely on their faith to get them through, even when they can't see the big picture.

> 'If any Muslim who suffers some calamity [problem] says that which Allah has commanded him: "We belong to Allah and to Him shall we return: O Allah, reward me for my affliction [problem] and give me something better in exchange for it", Allah will give him something better than it in exchange.'
> Hadith

? What links can be made between the quotation on this page and this photograph? Why do you think the Prophet Muhammad gave this advice to his followers?

a A young mother carries her malnourished child to a medical centre in Mogadishu, Somalia.

Case Study

I feel that when difficult things happen, I am being tested by Allah.

I think these tests verify your faith, requiring you to have patience in hard times, and to still have hope.

If there is a God, why does He let people suffer?

A lot of suffering can be related to the actions of humans, such as war. Islam encourages everyone to take responsibility for each other, and not doing this has bad consequences for this life.

Everyone has free will and sometimes people do bad things.

This life is not as important as life after death, when I hope to be with Allah in heaven. Heaven will not be a place of perfect peace if people who do bad things can get to heaven. When people are tested with suffering, it shows what they are really made of.

Good things come from suffering – it brings out positive characteristics in people because it lets them show compassion.

Reflection

What or who helped you through a difficult time? Why?

Activities

1. 'A good God would never allow people to suffer.' Debate this.

2. Which of the 99 names of Allah might help a Muslim who was suffering? Explain why.

3. Evaluate the Islamic idea that seeing life as a test makes suffering easier to bear. Express your response as a journal entry by a person who is going through a difficult time.

4. Think of an event from the news where something bad has happened and people have suffered. Choose one of the arguments on this page and suggest how it could be applied to that situation. Is it a good argument? What are its weaknesses? Explain your answer.

5. Discuss with a partner: Why do people remain religious despite so much suffering in the world?

4.5 Are We Responsible? Khalifah for Muslims

Learning Objectives

In this unit you will:

- analyse the Islamic belief that we are responsible for both the planet and other people
- explain the importance of **compassion** in Islam
- evaluate how far we are responsible for each other.

Starter

- What is most important to you about the world you live in? How do you show that it's important to you?

a

Muslims believe that the Earth is not here to be used solely as we wish. In Arabic, this is called **khalifah**, which means each person is a trustee of the Earth. They believe that humans must answer to Allah for their actions, and that every person is trusted to be responsible for not only themselves and their family, but also for the planet, animals, natural environment, and the rest of humanity.

Muslims believe that the planet Earth is very special, because of its natural laws and life forms. They believe that humans were created to care for, develop and look after the planet. Because of this, they think that the Earth should not be neglected or exploited, and that the delicate balance of the laws of nature must be maintained.

? Use a dictionary to look up the meanings of the words in the illustration. Then produce your own sentence explaining what Muslims believe their responsibilities are towards the Earth.

Useful Words

Khalifah The idea that Allah made people responsible for the Earth

Compassion Sympathizing with someone's situation with a desire to make it better

For an individual Muslim, being mindful of khalifah is about making sure that all of his or her resources are not left idle or wasted. So for example, if a Muslim hears about a family who has fallen on hard times and perhaps does not have furniture (such as a refugee), they will share what they have and try to find spare clothes for the children, furniture and so on. Many Muslims also share their wealth through giving to charity (see Unit 3.2).

Muslims believe that people should show compassion for others, and they are taught not to hold on to possessions that they do not need, and to use their time and skills to help others. They believe that what people claim to be theirs is not really true – it was loaned for their use by Allah, and along with it came responsibility for sharing.

This is not just about being generous. Muslims are all part of one ummah (community) and therefore believe other Muslims have a right to what they have.

b Muslim girls collecting donations for the charity Muslim Aid.

Reflection

Do you take any action to look after the world or other people around you? Why, or why not?

Activities

1 On a piece of paper, write a text message telling someone what they would need to do differently if they were responsible for the planet for future generations. Swap your text message with a partner and compare your ideas.

2 Do you think that humans are naturally selfish, or naturally caring and responsible? Why? Discuss your views with a partner.

3 Prepare to deliver a one-minute speech saying what you think the biggest problem facing the world is, and outlining one thing that an individual, community or government could do to help fix it.

4 'Even if you do not believe that Allah exists, being mindful of khalifah makes sense.' What do you think about this statement? Consider arguments for and against.

4.6 Does it Matter How the World was Created?

Learning Objectives

In this unit you will:

- examine Islamic views about creation theories and science
- evaluate the Islamic belief that Allah is Creator
- reflect on your own beliefs about religious and scientific explanations of creation.

Starter

- 'It doesn't matter how life began.' How far do you agree or disagree? Explain why.

People have been fascinated by the origins of the universe for centuries – how did it all begin?

Many scientists believe that the universe was formed billions of years ago, after a huge cosmic explosion called the Big Bang. It has been discovered that the universe is continually expanding – and, therefore, scientists believe that it must once have started at a central point.

a

b 〰️

The Qur'an says that Allah created the Earth and the heavens in six days. He created the night and the day, the sun and the moon; and He made them obey His commands. He made the wind blow and sent the rain to make plants grow. He provided everything that humans need and everything He made was good.

Allah then made people. He shaped Adam from clay and breathed His spirit into him. Allah then created Eve as a partner for Adam, and tested them by telling them that there was a tree with fruit that they must not eat.

'We have built the heaven with power, and We are expanding [it]'
The Qur'an 51:47

? Look at the two theories about the origins of the universe. What are their strengths and weaknesses?

Case Study

Mr Atcha is a scientist who believes that both science and his faith are important. He explains that the Qur'an contains information that is remarkably accurate, given the time when it was written.

I test the holy Qur'an against my knowledge of science. For example, the preciseness of the holy Qur'an to the up-to-date science of embryology.

Muslims believe that Allah created 'everything that is within the heavens and the Earth, and everything in between them'. Mrs Atcha explains that, on Earth, there are man-made things and God-made things. She believes that science is very important, and her children 'learn about and understand Islam through science'.

? Can a book that is centuries old reveal modern science?

Some Muslims, known as creationists, believe that the creation story in the Qur'an is literally true.

Other Muslims say that the Qur'an is written like a story to convey a message, and therefore could be compatible with modern scientific theories.

Reflection

Do you think that faith and science can work together?

Activities

1. Produce a collage to illustrate the Islamic idea that 'everything He made was good'.

2. Write five interesting questions to ask the Atcha family about how their faith relates to science. In pairs, see if you can guess what they might say.

3. How did the Earth begin? Draw three speech bubbles and – using the ideas from this Unit – write three contrasting viewpoints in them, including your own.

4.7 Is Killing Ever Justified? War and Capital Punishment

Learning Objectives

In this unit you will:

- learn about and explain Islamic attitudes to killing
- consider how and why war and **capital punishment** might be thought of as different to murder
- evaluate arguments for and against the taking of a life.

Starter

- Is it ever right to kill someone? Discuss your views with a partner.

Many Muslims believe that it's wrong to end a life, because Allah gives life and decides when people will die. However, according to the Qur'an, there are some occasions when killing is justified – but strict rules exist about the circumstances in these cases. The Qur'an allows capital punishment, because it puts people off committing serious crimes. However, before capital punishment can occur, there have to be many witnesses who can say truthfully that they saw the accused commit the crime.

The Qur'an says in 2:178 that a life may be taken for a life, but a killer who is forgiven by the victim's family can pay compensation instead, and their life will be spared. In fact, the victim's relatives are referred to as brothers – reminding Muslims of the bond between them and encouraging **mercy**.

? What are the arguments for and against capital punishment?

b Lindsay Sandiford was sentenced to death by firing squad in Bali in January 2013 for drug smuggling.

? The name of Allah 'the Merciful' (Ar Rahim) is repeated many times in Islamic prayer. When do you find it easy to show mercy to somebody who has done something bad to you?

a

Allah 'The Merciful' Ar Rahim

Because of media attention, some people mistakenly think that 'jihad' means that Muslims believe war is a good thing. Jihad actually means 'to struggle' in the cause of Allah, which can be wrongly interpreted (see Unit 4.3). In Islam, a religious authority must declare any war. The Qur'an also sets out conditions when fighting is acceptable – as a last resort.

c British soldiers in Basra, Iraq.

(see Unit 4.3)

Useful Words

Capital punishment Killing or executing somebody, using a country's legal process, for a serious crime they have committed

Mercy Showing forgiveness to somebody who you could punish

'To those against whom war is made, permission is given to fight, because they are wronged, and truly Allah is most powerful for their aid'
The Qur'an 22:39

'If they cease, let there be no hostility, except to those who practise oppression [on-going unfair treatment]'
The Qur'an 2:193

'If the enemy inclines towards peace, then you should also incline towards peace, and trust in Allah'
The Qur'an 8:61

? Choose one of the three quotations from the Qur'an and summarize it in your own words. Then evaluate it by coming up with arguments for and against what it suggests. Would you follow this advice?

Activities

1 Using the information in this unit, create an acrostic poem based on the word 'peace' – to show what Muslims believe about killing and war.

2 Write a short briefing sheet for a media journalist explaining the correct definition of the word 'jihad'.

3 'Capital punishment and war are no different to murder.' Using the information in this unit, as well as your own research, come up with arguments for and against this statement. Then prepare a piece in a format of your choice which sums up your own opinion.

Reflection

What are your guiding principles for this topic, and where do they come from?

Chapter 4 Assessment
Raising Questions, Exploring Answers

Objectives

- Interpret Islamic teachings about the purpose and meaning of life.
- Demonstrate empathy with Islamic views.
- Reflect on your place and responsibility in the world.

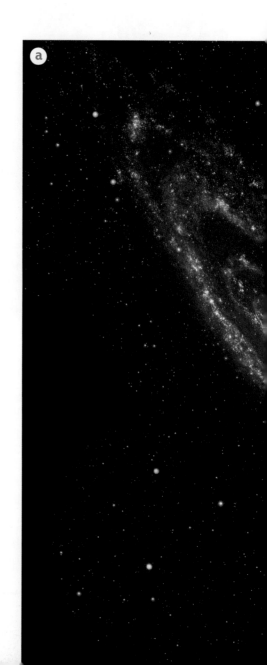
a

Task

'My place in the world.' Produce a draft for a web page or social networking profile page to show your philosophy about your existence – where you came from, why you are here, and how you relate to the world around you.

a Prepare: Using the ideas presented in Chapter 4, find key quotations and phrases that raise issues you would like to cover.

b Reflect: Use the above ideas as a mirror to reflect your own views, by deciding to what extent you agree or disagree with them. You could start each part of your web page with phrases like 'I agree with Muslims about … because …' or 'I disagree with Muslims about … because …'.

c Create: Use your preparation to design a web page.

A bit of guidance...

You are aiming to show your understanding of some religious (and philosophical) ideas, as well as giving your views. Don't just focus on what you think (and why), but also compare and contrast your views with those of Islam.

Hints and tips:

To help you tackle this task, you could do some of the following:

- Interview Muslims and other people about some of the issues raised in Chapter 4, and present these as features on your web page.
- Research Islamic environmental charities, and identify why they do their work.
- Research some Islamic contributions to science.

Guidance

What level are you aiming at? Have a look at the grid below to see what you need to do to achieve that level. What would you need to do to improve your work?

	I can...
Level 3	• use religious words to describe what Muslims believe • use a range of ways to express my agreement or disagreement • show how my beliefs influence my thoughts about the world I live in.
Level 4	• use a range of religious words to describe my philosophy on life • show understanding about the differences between my views and those of Islamic teachings • communicate my views effectively and with a range of reasons.
Level 5	• suggest reasons for my philosophy and whether I can relate to any Islamic ideas • use a wide range of religious and philosophical vocabulary • raise ultimate questions and show how consideration of these affects everyday life • apply my philosophy to the features I have created for my web page.
Level 6	• explain, interpret and evaluate some relevant quotations and examples from life or the media to justify and illustrate my response to the task • communicate my views creatively and persuasively, ensuring that all aspects of my understanding of the philosophy of existence are covered • highlight the challenges of living according to my philosophy.

Ready for more?

When you have completed this task, you can also work on your skills for Levels 6 and 7, and perhaps even higher. This is an extension task.

'Few of us live by our philosophy.' Do you agree?

- Reflect on the above statement and use your understanding from the task to inform a short essay or presentation.
- Consider evidence for and against the statement before reaching a conclusion.
- To achieve a high level, you will need to justify your arguments by referring to your views and those of Islam, as well as including relevant examples from life and the media (e.g. case studies of famous people who you believe do or don't live by their philosophy).

Islamic Beliefs in Action
5.1 Being a British Muslim

Learning Objectives

In this unit you will:

- explain what it means to be a British Muslim
- develop an understanding about how British Muslims link their identity and religion
- reflect on what 'British' means to you.

Starter

- What does it mean to be British? Write down three ideas and then, in groups of two or three, use your collected ideas to create a colourful mind-map.

When the early Muslims migrated to other countries, the Prophet Muhammad encouraged his followers to remain close to their faith, whilst still trying to fit in to their new communities. Many Muslims believe that they must obey the law of the country in which they live.

Some British Muslims might have moved to Britain from another country, but others might have lived in Britain for their entire lives. Some British Muslims do not even come from Muslim families, because they decided to convert to Islam as adults.

Whatever their heritage or family life, British Muslims try to make sure that they can practise their faith within the context of Britain. For example, many Muslim men will try to organize their working day on a Friday so that they can go to the mosque for jumu'ah prayers. In Muslim countries, this would not be an issue.

Today, around 4% of people in Britain are Muslim, and almost half of these live in London. There are a growing number of facilities for prayer and worship, as well as more halal meat shops and places to buy Islamic clothing, Qur'ans and so on.

? These are images of the Queen of England and Daniel Craig as James Bond. Who or what do you associate with the word 'British'?

Case Study

The extended Atcha family talk about their experiences of being Muslims in Britain.

> To be Muslim is to submit your life to Allah. To be British is somebody who makes their home in Britain. I may not accept everything that people around me do, but I do consider this my home. This is where I was born. This is where we are raising our children.

> For me, being British is mixing with people and being part of the community. There are certain things I can't do, for example I've never been to a nightclub and I've never drunk alcohol. I know it plays a huge role in the community. Those things I don't do, but I do everything else. I've got friends of all different races and I'm part of the usual culture, like eating fish and chips, etc!

> **?** Many Muslims shop for groceries at halal stores. What 'British' things do you think a Muslim can or cannot do?

> I think being British is having to follow the British law, and we look after the country because it's our own country.

A.K. HALAL MEAT
WHOLESALE & RETAIL   020 7738 6622

Activities

1. Imagine that you are a town planner. What facilities would you include for Muslims?

2. Create a guide for a Muslim who is planning to move to Britain, which explains British culture and what he or she may have to consider about being Muslim in Britain.

3. How easy is it to be spiritual in modern society? Discuss your thoughts with a partner.

Reflection

How important is it for a person to feel 'British' when they live in Britain?

5.2 Same Difference? Men and Women in Islam

Learning Objectives

In this unit you will:

- evaluate the rights and duties of men and women in Islam
- analyse the Islamic belief that Allah created men and women equal but different
- reflect on whether society stereotypes people by gender.

Starter

- What do you think of when someone says 'Muslim woman'? In pairs, note down your thoughts.

Many Muslims believe that, during his lifetime, the Prophet Muhammad saw that women were very badly treated. Through the revelations in the Qur'an and by his own personal behaviour, he made it clear that women were equal to men.

The role of women in Islam is a topic of much debate, often because of the way that many Muslim women dress (see Unit 3.6). The requirements of Islam are sometimes confused with cultural issues. Many Muslim women in Britain are from other countries, and the ways in which they practise Islam can depend on how things are done in their home cultures. Different cultures interpret 'modesty' in different ways.

'It is He [Allah] who created you from a single person.'
The Qur'an 7:189

'For Muslim men and women
For believing men and women
For devout men and women
For true men and women
For men and women who are patient and constant
For men and women who humble themselves
For men and women who give in charity
For men and women who fast and deny themselves
For men and women who guard their chastity
and for men and women who engage much in Allah's praise,
For them has Allah prepared forgiveness and great reward.'
The Qur'an 33:35

Many Muslims believe that Allah created men and women to complement each other and work together, in partnership. Verses of the Qur'an often refer to the nature of men and women – making general comments about ways in which they typically behave (as do some modern relationship guidance books). While some roles are given to men and women as their 'responsibility', in practice the work is often shared – even if one person has the job of making sure that it's done.

Responsibilities for men and women

Muslims believe that women's education is important, and also that a woman is responsible for ensuring that, if she has children, they receive moral and religious education.

Muslims believe that modesty is required of both men and women and, whether a woman is dressed modestly or not, it is a man's responsibility to respect women.

Children are very important in Islam. Many Muslim women work, but most would say that the welfare of their family comes first. The Qur'an says that men should support the family financially.

? What do you think of the responsibilities outlined in the boxes above? Why might some Muslim men and women decide to interpret these differently?

b In Islam, men and women are equal but often have different roles.

Activities

1 If men and women are equal in Islam, why do they often look different? In pairs, come up with interesting questions to ask Mr and Mrs Atcha (pictured) on this topic.

2 Read the Qur'an 33:35 (on the opposite page) and consider why the phrase 'for men and women' is repeated so many times.

3 **a** 'No matter what religion says, most cultures value men more than women.' Discuss this statement, considering different sides of the argument.

b What do you associate with the words 'men' and 'women'? Compare your thoughts with a partner.

Reflection

Do you think that everyone in your family takes their fair share of responsibility? How does this work – or not? What jobs and responsibilities do you have? Do you always carry them out?

5.3 Nature or Nurture? The Muslim Family

Learning Objectives

In this unit you will:

- learn about and explain the Islamic attitude to the family
- evaluate how Muslims respond to the challenges faced by families in modern society
- reflect on whether these values should apply to everyone.

Starter

- Families are made up in many different ways. Who do you think of as family?

Muslims value family life and most would say that 'family' includes their extended family – grandparents and other relatives. Islamic laws and Sunnah support the importance of family.

As well as this, family in Islam is used to refer to all Muslims worldwide, and Muslims often call each other (even strangers) brother or sister. This is the ummah and the community tries to take care of each other.

> '*Be careful of your duty to Allah and be fair and just to your children.*'
> Hadith

? How would a Muslim apply the advice in the quotation to family life?

? What can you see in this picture? What words would you use to describe this family?

Muslims in Britain may face issues that they might not in countries where there is a majority of Muslims:

Aims of a Muslim family	Issues in Britain
Raise children with Islamic values	Not everyone in Britain shares the same values
Educate children in Islam	Finding time, and those who can teach well
Encourage children to grow up to make good choices about relationships	Children wanting to fit in to another culture, for example by accepting the practice of 'dating', even though many Muslims believe they should not do this
Have fun together	Long working hours; busy lives
Spending the main religious festivals/ events together	Many relatives live far away, and working hours do not always fit in with festivals
'Be kind to your parents, whether one or both of them live to an old age.' The Qur'an 17:23	Busy working lives, and the challenges of caring for elderly relatives
Bury family members in accordance with Islam; personally take care of the funeral rituals	A lack of facilities for Islamic burial

b Muslims believe it is very important to honour the elderly.

Reflection

Religious people sometimes say 'The family that prays together stays together'. What does this mean? Do you agree? Why or why not?

Activities

1. Choose one of the aims and issues in the table above and write a letter to an advice column explaining your problem and seeking help. Swap with someone in the class and answer each other's letters.

2. Many Muslims think that the family is the first place where children can experience and develop the qualities that Allah wants them to have. Look at the 'aims' in the table. What qualities are families trying to develop in them?

3. 'The world would be fixed if we all treated each other as family.' Can you think of an argument that agrees and one that disagrees with this? Then, express your own opinion creatively, either as a poem, collage or poster.

5.4 How Do We Know What Is Right?

Learning Objectives

In this unit you will:

- learn why Muslims believe that life is special and sacred
- explain how this influences Muslims when making decisions
- reflect on who or what you turn to for ethical decisions.

Starters

- Identify three things that are special about being human. Share and compare your thoughts with a partner.

In ethical decisions – decisions about right and wrong – many Muslims start by looking at what is said in the Qur'an.

Guiding principles in the Qur'an

- Life is sacred because it comes from Allah.
- People have value over and above the physical body.
- Muslims should make decisions based on what Allah wants.
- Allah does not send a soul more than it can bear.
- Look after orphans.

Useful Words

Euthanasia The act of killing someone painlessly, usually to end their suffering; this is illegal in Britain

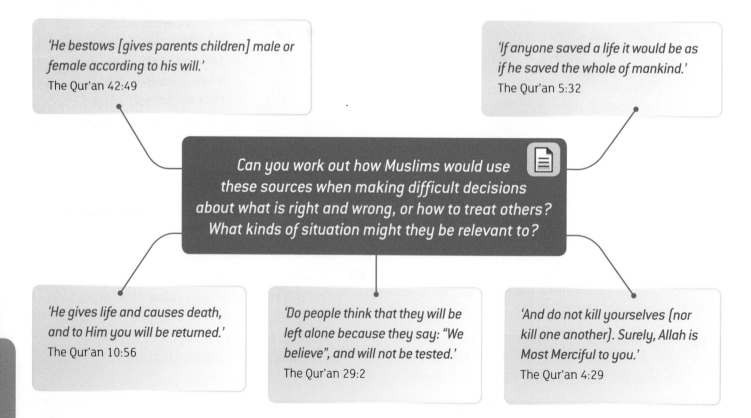

'He bestows [gives parents children] male or female according to his will.'
The Qur'an 42:49

'If anyone saved a life it would be as if he saved the whole of mankind.'
The Qur'an 5:32

Can you work out how Muslims would use these sources when making difficult decisions about what is right and wrong, or how to treat others? What kinds of situation might they be relevant to?

'He gives life and causes death, and to Him you will be returned.'
The Qur'an 10:56

'Do people think that they will be left alone because they say: "We believe", and will not be tested.'
The Qur'an 29:2

'And do not kill yourselves (nor kill one another). Surely, Allah is Most Merciful to you.'
The Qur'an 4:29

Modern life is very different from the Prophet Muhammad's time. Nowadays, science has made so many things possible. For example, someone might consider donating their organs after death to help save other people's lives.

Muslims believe that even though the Qur'an and Hadiths do not deal directly with these issues, relevant guidance can be found in them. Where a clear answer is given, it's seen as a law and Muslims follow that first – such as the law about not killing others.

Even if somebody has a poor quality of life (for example, because they experience daily pain), their life is still thought of as sacred.

Therefore, many Muslims say that **euthanasia** is wrong. By relieving someone's suffering in this way, they would fail the test sent by Allah to live according to the Qur'an.

Muslims also believe that everyone has a conscience – an inner voice – and if they listen to it properly, it will help them to make the right decisions. Whilst many Muslims agree that scientific developments are a good thing, it is down to individual believers to search for guidance when the right decision isn't clear.

? The author Terry Pratchett was diagnosed with Alzheimer's in 2008, and has taken an active role in the media in promoting euthanasia and a change to the law in the UK. Can you find out more about his campaign? Why does he feel so strongly about the issue?

Activities

1. Which of the statements opposite do you think are clear laws and which are more general principles?

2. Put the following in order of importance for where a Muslim should look for guidance: cultural traditions, family, Qur'an, Hadiths. Label each one with your reasoning.

3. Tell a partner three things that make you think we do, or do not, have a conscience.

4. 'Euthanasia is never the right decision.' Do you agree or disagree? Explain your reasons.

Reflection

What or who influences your opinions and decisions about big issues?

Learning Objectives

In this unit you will:

- explore the perceptions of Islam in the media
- examine what Muslims think about how they are shown in the media
- reflect on why stereotypes sometimes exist.

Starter

- What does it mean to 'stereotype' someone?

It is sometimes said that bad news sells newspapers. Since the events of 9/11, Islam has had a lot of media coverage. Muslims all over the world were shocked by the events.

Some feel that 'terrorists hijacked my religion' – meaning that they carried out acts which are against the basic teachings of Islam, whilst claiming that they did it in the name of Islam. As a result of this, Muslims are sometimes regarded with suspicion, or treated badly.

A recent study showed that a lot of coverage of Islam in the press since 2000 has been negative, and also presents a one-sided view of Muslims. It often also stereotypes Muslims by showing pictures of them protesting, or wearing strict dress, or outside police stations. This can lead to **Islamophobia**. Other surveys have shown that this is not how the British public in general see Muslims.

Useful Words

Islamophobia Prejudice against Muslims because of their faith, including a hatred of Islam that leads to fear and dislike of Muslims

? What would you say to someone who had picked up negative perceptions of Islam from the media? What would you say to the newspapers?

Case Study

Mrs Atcha talks about how she feels living as a Muslim in Britain: 'I don't think the public sees me as I see myself. People will often treat me differently, but I've found that – as soon as I start communicating – people's perception of me changes.'

Mr Atcha spent some time working in a hospital, and found that his patients 'would initially have a very significant reaction' against him when they first saw him. Like his wife, he found that 'by the end of the treatment, it's a thank you; it would go from a very cold start, to a very warm finish'.

When it comes to stereotyping Muslims, Mr Atcha believes that it's important that people understand no two Muslims are the same: 'there are 1.5 billion Muslims and, as Malcolm X said, they could be whiter than white or blacker than black. They could come from Africa, America, or they could be native English Muslims, or come from Australia. There are Muslims all over the world.'

? What do you think this case study says about the people that Mr and Mrs Atcha often come into contact with?

Activities

1. Write a letter from Mr Atcha to a newspaper editor, describing the impact that negative media coverage has had on his life.

2. In pairs, produce the front page of a newspaper that aims to balance up the media coverage of Islam. You could include articles on a range of issues, e.g. why Muslims do not approve of images of Allah or Muhammad, Islamic clothing, or halal food.

3. 'Newspapers aren't responsible for presenting a balanced viewpoint. They just report what people want to read about.' In pairs, consider the arguments for and against this statement.

Reflection

Have you ever stereotyped someone without meaning to? Why did this happen?

Learning Objectives

In this unit you will:

- explore how Islam regards other faiths
- examine the values that Islam shares with other faiths
- reflect on the benefits of having many friends from different backgrounds.

Starters

- How many people of different faiths do you know? See if you can draw a pie chart that shows what percentages of people from different faiths you know.

Case Study

Aminah Atcha believes that it's really important to have a range of friends who all believe different things. Whilst she has lots of Muslim friends, she also has friends who are '**atheist**, Christian, Jewish, or from a Hindu background'.

In particular, she comments on some of the similarities between her Jewish and Christian friends.

For all of her friends, whether they are religious or not, Aminah says 'the thing that brings us all together is the desire to be a good person'.

However, Aminah acknowledges that there are some differences.

We all have the Ten Commandments, and all our three sacred books promote the respect of others, being a good human being, being good to your parents, and doing charity work.

I don't party or go to pubs, and I think that can sometimes separate us, but as time has gone on me and my friends have learned to do activities I can get more involved in.

? Islam is one of the Abrahamic faiths and shares some key figures with Judaism and Christianity. What similarities and differences have you seen as you have studied Islam?

Useful Words

Atheist A person who does not believe in the existence of any god

The verse on the right was given to the Prophet Muhammad to show the importance of teaching the early Muslims to be faithful to their beliefs. It teaches that they should maintain their faith, even when they are separated from their Islamic community. Many Muslims interpret this to mean that they should live in harmony with non-Muslims, and not to worry about what other people are doing around them – they should continue to focus on following their own path, wherever they might be.

a An interfaith group gathers to show unity and to condemn anti-Islamic attitudes in 2011.

> 'To each of you We [Allah] prescribed a law and a method. Had Allah willed, He would have made you one nation [united in religion], but [He intended] to test you in what He has given you; so race to [all that is] good. To Allah is your return all together, and He will [then] inform you concerning that over which you used to differ.'
>
> The Qur'an 5:48

? In pairs, put the quotation into your own words. Why might living amongst many different people be a form of 'test' for Muslims?

Reflection

What are the advantages of having more friends with different viewpoints?

? Although many Muslims celebrate the similarities they have with other faiths, they also acknowledge that other faiths would not agree that Muhammad was the last Prophet, and that the Qur'an was the direct word to him from Allah. Why do you think many Muslims support interfaith events, if there is disagreement on such important issues?

Activities

1 In pairs, hot-seat Aminah about the positive aspects – and also the challenges – of having friends with different belief systems.

2 How could meeting people from different belief systems change someone's view about them?

3 Imagine if the world were 'one nation, united in religion'. Considering both the pros and cons of this, express your response in a creative format of your choice, for example, a poem, collage or speech.

Islamic Beliefs in Action

Objectives

- Demonstrate knowledge of how Muslims apply rules in their lives.

- Apply knowledge to designing facilities and services for Muslims and making sure their needs are met.

Task

Imagine that you are the mayor of your town, and you have been given the task of improving the facilities for Muslims. Using what you've learned, produce an action plan for your town, with reasons to back up your suggestions. What new or improved facilities or services would be needed?

A bit of guidance...

This task will help you to showcase your skills of empathy and application, as well as your ability to record decisions clearly and demonstrate thinking skills in your decision-making processes.

You are aiming to show your understanding of the laws and habits of Muslims that you have studied. Don't just focus on what you think (and why), but also on finding and using appropriate evidence that you can explain and expand upon as reasoning for the decisions you make.

Hints and tips:

To help you tackle this task, you could do some of the following:

- List all of the Islamic rules you know about.

- Use examples from the news, TV and 'real life' to support your views, as well as from a range of other sources.

- Research your local area to find out what facilities are already provided for Muslims and whether they can be improved.

Guidance

What level are you aiming at? Have a look at the grid below to see what you need to do to achieve that level. What would you need to do to improve your work?

	I can...
Level 3	• describe what guides Muslims in their daily lives and decision-making, recognizing similarities and differences between Islamic lifestyles and my own.
Level 4	• use relevant quotations and religious words to describe an Islamic lifestyle • show understanding of the importance of following the Prophet Muhammad's lifestyle and teachings, and the impact of this.
Level 5	• identify, explain and evaluate some relevant quotations and examples from life or the media to illustrate my interpretation of Islamic rules • communicate my views creatively and with a range of religious reasons.
Level 6	• use religious and philosophical vocabulary to relate actions to key Islamic beliefs • express insight into the complications of having to balance lots of rules • consider the challenges of building an Islamic community where the existing rules may be different • communicate my views creatively and persuasively.

Ready for more?

When you have completed this task, you can also work on your skills for Levels 6 and 7, and perhaps even higher. This is an extension task.

'People migrating to a country should always try to fit in.'
Do you agree?

- Reflect upon the above statement and use your understanding from the task to inform a short essay (two or three paragraphs).
- Consider evidence for and against the statement before reaching a conclusion.
- To achieve a high level, you will need to justify your arguments by referring to what it means to live in a multicultural society – and the importance of beliefs and values to people.

Glossary

Abrahamic faiths Those faiths (Islam, Judaism and Christianity) that acknowledge Abraham as a common origin

Adhan When a person called the Mu'adhin says a prayer calling Muslims to pray; in many countries it is played through loudspeakers from the minaret (tower) of a mosque, so that everyone can hear, stop what they are doing and pray

Akhirah Eternal life

Alhamdulillah Thanks be to Allah

Allah The Arabic name for God, used in Islam

Atheist A person who does not believe in the existence of any god

Capital punishment Killing/ executing somebody, using a country's legal process, for a serious crime they have committed

Compassion Sympathizing with someone's situation with a desire to make it better

Du'a Personal prayer

Eid-ul-Adha Festival of sacrifice

Eid-ul-Fitr The celebration at the end of Ramadan, after a month of fasting

Euthanasia The act of killing someone painlessly, usually to end their suffering; this is illegal in Britain

Gospels The four books at the start of the New Testament in the Bible

Hadith The collected sayings of the Prophet Muhammad

Hajj The fifth pillar of Islam; a pilgrimage to Makkah that Muslims should try to complete at least once in their lives, if they are able

Halal Lawful

Haram Unlawful

Hijab Muslim woman's head, hair and chest covering

Idol worship The worship of statues, or things that are not God

Imam A religious leader in Islam

Inshaa Allah If God wills it

Islamophobia Prejudice against Muslims because of their religion, including a hatred of Islam that leads to fear and dislike of Muslims

Jama'ah Local mosque community of Muslims

Jihad Personal struggle (the 'greater' jihad); holy war or struggle (the 'lesser' jihad)

Ka'bah A cube-shaped structure in the centre of the grand mosque in Makkah; it does not contain anything to worship – in fact, Muhammad removed all 'idols' from it

Khalifah The idea that Allah made people responsible for the Earth

Khutbah Sermon at Friday prayers

Makkah The holiest city of Islam; Muslims face towards Makkah when they pray

Mercy Showing forgiveness to somebody who you could punish

Modesty Decency of behaviour, speech and dress

Mosque clothes Traditional clothes worn by some Muslim men for going to the mosque (an Islamic place of worship)

Persecution Hostility towards and ill treatment of an individual or group, often because of their race, religion or politics

Pilgrimage A special journey with spiritual intention

Polytheism Belief in more than one God

Qur'an The holy text in Islam

Quraysh A tribe in Makkah in Muhammad's lifetime

Qurbani The meat of animals sacrificed at Eid-ul-Adha that are shared with family and the poor

Ramadan The ninth month of the Islamic year; the time when the Qur'an was revealed to the Prophet Muhammad (and now the most holy month)

Revelation Revealing or showing communication from Allah

Righteousness Being moral or acting properly

Sadaqah Any good deed done for the sake of Allah, rather than selfish reasons

Salah The second pillar of Islam; Islamic prayer carried out five times each day

Sawm Fasting; going without food or drink from dawn to sunset

Secular Without religious reference; non-religious

Shahadah The words Muslims use to confirm their belief and to declare that they are Muslim

Shari'ah Islamic law derived by scholars from the Qur'an, Sunnah and Hadith

Shaytan Satan, or the devil

Shirk Believing in something other than Allah at the time of death, or saying that Allah has an equal

Subhah These are beads used to keep count of personal prayers. Some have 99 beads and some 33, so they are especially useful for reciting the 99 names of Allah

Sunnah Actions and teaching of the Prophet Muhammad

Tayyib Pure

The Night Journey A miraculous spiritual journey, during which the Prophet Muhammad was taken from Makkah to 'the farthest place of worship' (The Qur'an 17:1)

Ummah Worldwide community of Muslims

Zakah The third pillar of Islam; payment of 2.5% of annual savings

Index